DRIVE YOURSELF
SUCCESSFUL

DRIVE YOURSELF

SUCCESSFUL

11 INNER STATES TO
PERSONAL EMPOWERMENT

RACHEL LYNN

SOUND WISDOM
P.O. Box 310
Shippensburg, PA 17257-0310

For more information on publishing and distribution rights, call 717-530-2122 or info@soundwisdom.com.

Quantity Sales. Special discounts are available on quantity purchases by corporations, associations, and others. For details, contact the Sales Department at Sound Wisdom.

While efforts have been made to verify information contained in this publication, neither the author nor the publisher assumes any responsibility for errors, inaccuracies, or omissions.

While this publication is chock-full of useful, practical information, it is not intended to be legal or accounting advice. All readers are advised to seek competent lawyers and accountants to follow laws and regulations that may apply to specific situations.

The reader of this publication assumes responsibility for the use of the information. The author and publisher assume no responsibility or liability whatsoever on the behalf of the reader of this publication.

ISBN 13 TP: 978-1-937879-67-9
ISBN 13 Ebook: 978-1-937879-68-6

For Worldwide Distribution, Printed in the U.S.A.
1 2 3 4 5 6 7 8 / 20 19 18 17

Cover/Jacket designer: Eileen Rockwell
Interior designer: Terry Clifton

DEDICATION

This book is dedicated to all the beautiful souls who had the courage to seek help and who entrusted me to serve as your counselor. Each of you taught me empathy, understanding, compassion, and how to help make a positive difference in the lives of others. You are the inspiration for this book which will reach many others who share life's struggles and adversities.

ACKNOWLEDGMENTS

I offer my sincere gratitude to my son, Ryan, who has shown me what unconditional love is and for being my reason to follow my dreams; my mother and stepfather, Jenny and Charles Carter, for making me the person I am today and holding me accountable; to Alan Forrest for inspiring and teaching me how to be a helper; to Don Green for your mentorship, guidance, and for believing in me; to my friend, Lanna, for your support, encouragement, and mastermind alliance; and to my soul mate, John, who is my best friend and my rock. To everyone else who encouraged and supported me during this process, I extend my sincere gratitude and deepest appreciation.

CONTENTS

PREFACE

Welcome to my book, *Drive Yourself Successful: 11 Inner States to Personal Empowerment!* The following pages have the potential to position you in the driver's seat of your own life if you take the wheel and embrace your journey. My name is Rachel Lynn, and my experience as a licensed professional counselor has equipped me with firsthand knowledge of what keeps people's gearshifts stuck in park, as well as what is necessary to shift back into drive. Through my work as a therapist, I have witnessed the struggles, obstacles, and anchors that hold people back from living their lives to their true potential. I have witnessed people live as passive passengers in their own lives, paralyzed by fear and self-doubt due to life experiences and negative thought patterns. I have also experienced my own adversities in which I have personally followed the paths I have shared in this book to not only get through life's trying times but also to use them as fuel to thrive.

In addition to experiencing my own struggles and witnessing those of others, I have observed what it takes to triumph over unfortunate circumstances, self-limiting beliefs, and negative experiences and become empowered to persevere. I have facilitated growth in many individuals by assisting them in shifting their mind-set, challenging irrational beliefs, reframing perceptions, refocusing emotional energy, and helping them to develop a vision for themselves and their future. As a result of my experience in working with so many amazing individuals who refused to stay a passive passenger in their own lives, I have written this book to encompass the many common experiences that people share and have provided you with the specific tools for achieving happiness and success, despite your past or current life circumstances. I have found that the use of analogies works well in helping others gain clear perspectives and insight into their lives, and I have written this book using the analogy of a car, something that is relatable to most people. I will teach you how to reprogram your guidance system to transform negative life experiences into fuel to accelerate you toward the life you desire. When you learn to practice the 11 inner states shared in this book, you will find yourself cruising through life feeling empowered, happy, peaceful, and successful. Welcome to your new journey and the transition into the driver's seat of your life!

INTRODUCTION

Have you ever reached a point where, no matter what you do to establish a sense of direction and control in life, it seems other people or circumstances are driving your life in one direction or another? Do you ever feel your life is directed by the actions of others and/or by seemingly uncontrollable situations and not by your own thoughts, ideas, and actions? This can become extremely frustrating and depressing and may lead to a sense of helplessness and hopelessness about the future.

Unfortunately, most people give up on their dreams, giving in to others' words and actions, or simply surrender to unpleasant circumstances believing this is just the way it is and it's never going to get better. If you believe this, it's exactly what you'll get—a dead end—and, therefore, you reinforce negative beliefs that are perception and not reality.

You see, what we perceive becomes our reality—whether accurate or not. It is sad that most people never realize that what they think about and believe determines the quality of both their life's journey and final destination. Thoughts directly lead to feelings, and feelings lead to actions—or lack thereof. Therefore, if you're in a negative mind-set, you will only see and feel the negative and fail to take appropriate action for improvement.

Picture yourself driving to a place you've always dreamed of visiting. You're excited about the trip and can't wait to arrive. You stop at a red light. Suddenly, someone yanks open your car door, pushes you into the passenger seat, and begins recklessly driving your car in the opposite direction of your destination. That person, now in complete control of your car, isn't holding you at gunpoint, hasn't made any threats, and yet has completely taken the driver's seat, determining your destination. Envision this—you have allowed this person to take the wheel of your life, and you somehow believe this person knows the best route—to get you to *their* desired location! With an overwhelming sense of powerlessness over where you are going, you have willingly handed over your keys and left your life's journey up to someone else. Your once desired destination has now given way to someone else's control without you even putting up a fight!

So what now? Basically, you have two choices: a) you can remain a passive passenger, always at the mercy of the whims of another or a victim of unfortunate circumstances, or b) you can take back the driver's seat and become an assertive driver!

The first step in regaining the driver's seat is to acknowledge and realize you do not have to sit in the passenger seat and watch the scenery of life pass by from others' perspectives. You can't change what you don't acknowledge. Once you acknowledge that this isn't how life has to be, you empower yourself to take action and get back on the path to success.

Once you train your thoughts to focus on your true potential—disregarding the lies and negative fuel you've been using that has kept your gearshift stuck in park or has spun you 100 miles an hour in the wrong direction—your motivation accelerates and you shift into "drive." When this happens, opportunities for self-growth and success are exponential, and you'll find yourself able to travel toward goals and aspirations you've always dreamed of reaching. You've probably heard the phrase "life happens." Well, sometimes, life "doesn't happen" for many people. Sadly, some people merely exist—like a parked car with a dead battery and flat tires—never realizing that, with a little work and maintenance, they could travel great distances.

There are several areas to consider that will help you gain perspective on your life's direction. It's not about whether you can or you can't; it's a matter of whether you *believe* you can or can't. Life is much like a car if you think about it. It's a vessel to get you from point "A" to point "B"; it requires regular maintenance and putting your foot down on negativity in order to accelerate; what you put into it is what you get out of it; and *only the driver* holds the key to where it goes. This book will spark your inner drive and steer you straight to success in all areas of life!

Clean Out Your Trunk

For many people, life events, losses, failures, and poor relationships paralyze them from moving forward and achieving their goals and even depress their desire for a better life. Oftentimes, people give way to the irrational belief that, because of past experiences, they don't deserve a good life, to be happy, or to have goals. So many people remain in "park" because of the past and cling to negative beliefs they are convinced are true, even though they're not.

There's a big difference between perception and reality. However, one's perception *becomes* their reality whether factual or not. Your feelings and behaviors are a direct result of your perceptions. If you consistently feel awful about yourself, you can bet you have some stinking thinking going on!

As a human being, you are unique and were created with a purpose that only *you* can fulfill. When you allow your mind to be permeated with negative information about who you are and who you aren't, it's like having a brand-new car and choosing not to take the key and go for a spin because you believe that particular brand isn't capable of your commute and you're certain it will break down at some point.

Think about the trunk of your car. There may be things stored in there you don't see on a daily basis, yet you know they're there, and they go with you wherever you go. This works the same way with our thoughts and memories—words others have said to us, our experiences, past actions that have skewed our perception of ourselves and fill us with doubt about our abilities. While these experiences collect over time and remain stored in the trunk of our memory, we are very aware of their presence and feel them everywhere we go, which negatively affects many areas of our lives.

Sometimes the weight stored in our trunks feels as if it's too much for us to haul around. Perhaps you believe that trying to lift the weighty items stored in your trunk in order to clear it out would be too exhausting or that you're not capable of doing the work necessary to clean out your trunk. Therefore, you travel through life carrying the weight of the past, lugging it with you wherever you go, and not allowing room for new experiences that reflect your true abilities.

Just because you do not acknowledge the weight in the trunk, it doesn't mean it's going to clear out on its own. This requires work from you, and sometimes it does get more difficult before it gets easier. But, the important thing to focus your attention on is the fact that, at some point, life *will* get easier,

Delight in Living

815-459-5161

and you'll be able to face each day free of the weights you've been carrying in your trunk for so long. Once you begin to clear these items out of your trunk, you will begin to accelerate in a positive direction.

What is it from your past that's stored in your mind and keeps you a passenger in life, decreasing your sense of self-worth and depleting your motivation to pursue your dreams? Here are some examples of the types of things often stored in the trunks of many people's "cars."

WORDS

Words can have a paralyzing impact on our thoughts and self-beliefs, especially if those words are negative and they come from parents, family, intimate partners, or close friends. These words determine how you define yourself. The way you define yourself leads you to either pursue your dreams and goals or give them up. Perhaps you've been told you will never amount to anything, or you'll never achieve the dreams you've voiced to others. Perhaps you've been told you're not smart enough, talented enough, attractive enough, or worthy enough to accomplish your dreams. Many people have been shunned by their families for voicing their attempts to set goals, being told that they are "getting above their raising."

Ironically enough, there are many people who fear success just as much as, or more than, failure. Sometimes, others don't want to see you successful because it makes them feel worse about themselves or they're afraid they'll lose you in some way. Many times, people will attempt to hold you back because they lack the confidence and initiative to do things for themselves.

Should you relate to this experience, I encourage you to consider the source and ask yourself the following questions: "Is this person's comment in my best interests?" "Is this person successful in life?" "Does this person have my genuine interests in mind?" "Is this person supportive?" "Could this person be jealous?" "What does this person stand to lose should I be successful in achieving my goals?"

A lot of people offer opinions and/or advice, and often we ask for those opinions and advice. However, we must use caution when doing so, as words are only words until we provide them with emotional meaning. By seeking the advice of others or receiving others' unsolicited advice or negative comments, we set ourselves up for what has the potential to be the beginning of the end. This is the point where we allow others to sneak into the driver's seat of our lives with minimal or no confrontation. Why allow someone else to be the decision maker of your life or determine the direction you should follow? Ask yourself if you're willingly handing over the keys to someone else and letting them decide your destiny. As long as you allow others to control your self-esteem, your life direction, and your thoughts, you are weighed down, unable to move forward and live life to your true potential. Your trunk will become so bogged down with the weight of negativity that your car will refuse to shift into drive.

Consider negative words as a positive sign you're on to something big! For example, suppose you share your plans and ideas with another person. This person believes you have the potential and capabilities to achieve your goals and, for whatever reason, begins to feel threatened by your potential success. What do you think their response will be? It is highly likely this person will discourage you or attempt to hinder your progress. If you allow this discouragement and hindrance into your thinking and start to believe it yourself, there is a very strong chance you will give up on your ideas and discard your plans. At this point, because you have allowed another's discouraging and negative comments to steer your thinking into a cesspool, this stinking thinking becomes accepted and reinforced in your mind. As a result, the negativity of someone else has infected you, and now you believe it to be true in your own mind when in reality it is absolutely false!

Please remember, you cannot succeed if you do not try, and you will only reach the level of success you believe you can achieve! When you uphold negative, self-defeating thinking, you start down the road of believing you're a failure, incapable, and worthless, and if you travel this road long enough, you won't even attempt any positive turn of the wheel in the direction of your life unless you are shaken out of that negative belief fog.

We have a tendency to create our own sinkholes. Remember, just because someone says something, it doesn't make it true! Words are simply words until we attach meaning to them. If you believe the negative and derogatory statements of others, you've seated yourself as a passive passenger on the road of life, allowing others to dictate your worth and abilities, thus robbing you of your personal power. Thus, you've given all the power to others to dictate your life's journey and final destination. When you believe the falsehoods and misinterpretations of others, it's like having an eight-cylinder engine and letting a four-cylinder engine smoke you! You are left defeated and completely exhausted! The worst part is that you chose not to put your foot down to negativity and accelerate toward your desired destination.

Hopefully, you are fired up and looking closely at how you have given others' words power over you, and you know you now have to take back control of your life and change gears in a new direction. Keep in mind, you can't change what you're not aware of or what you don't acknowledge or own, and because you have now been made aware, it's time to start by challenging each negative comment you have been told and replacing it with a healthier, more realistic statement.

For example, let's take the comment, "You will never succeed." You could replace this statement with positive affirmations such as, "I am perfectly capable of achieving the goals I have set for myself." "My success or failure will be based solely on *my* efforts and not because of someone else's negative comments or opinion."

I would encourage you to stop here and make a list of all the negative statements you can remember that someone has said to you. After you have completed that, replace those negative statements with new, self-assuring affirmations similar to those stated in the above paragraph.

The next step is to read aloud, if possible, these new, positive affirmations to yourself every day. Keep stating them over and over to yourself in your thoughts, as this will activate auto-suggestion—a way of conditioning or reprogramming your subconscious, which is the part of your mind that's got all the resources to make things happen for you. Post these affirmations somewhere you can consistently see them so they serve as a constant reminder of your true potential and refusal to let others' words dictate your life's direction.

Another set of words that may be stored in your trunk are words you have said to someone else that caused hurt and emotional pain to them. Sometimes, we never have the chance to apologize. This can create guilt that lasts a lifetime. Guilt follows its victim wherever they go and diminishes the horsepower needed to travel life's journey freely. For some, they continually travel down the same dead-end street with nothing but a worn path of self-inflicted, emotional torment that leads to nowhere. If this is you, now is the time to *forgive yourself!* You do not have to carry the burden of guilt forever. Stop punishing yourself for past mistakes! *Everyone* makes mistakes, and if we are honest, we've all said or done things to others we wish we could take back. All of us get lost on our journey at times or take the wrong street, but we don't deserve a *lifetime* of self-inflicted abuse, punishment, and self-sabotage because of this. You wouldn't continue to criticize the driver who temporarily lost his way, so don't do this to yourself. Let it go! Stop, turn around, and move on! Take your eyes off the rearview mirror and focus only on the good things you said or did for the person with whom your words created hurt and pain. Don't keep looking back at the past. You can't move forward if the gearshift is in reverse!

LOSS

Losing someone you love can be heartbreaking. But choosing to withdraw from life and remain parked in your garage because you feel guilty for being alive is completely irrational. So many times, people idle in park or become stuck or broken down due to their experience of loss.

Grief is a normal process, and everyone grieves in different ways. However, allowing guilt to debilitate you is like parking a

$100,000 car when the tires become worn instead of purchasing new tires and getting back out on the road of life. Remember the statement made in the introduction of this book? Our thoughts *directly* create our feelings, and our feelings control our behaviors.

If you've thought it's not fair for you to go on living and enjoying life because your loved one is gone, you will never be happy. It's like locking yourself in the trunk of their car—it's not good for you or them. Unfortunately, many people develop irrational thoughts such as this after the loss of a loved one. If you believe it, it becomes your reality, and your actions *will* align with your beliefs. This kind of thinking leads to a life of unnecessary misery, guilt, and self-defeat. Most likely, this is *not* what your loved one would want for you! What would your lost loved one say to you if they could see you in this state of mind and being? Do you think they would want you to give up on life because they are no longer with you? Do you think they would want you to stay hidden in the trunk of their car fueling yourself with blame and guilt? I can tell you with certainty, absolutely *not!* However, guilt, hurt, and pain will be your reality as long as you cling to this belief.

So, how do you rebuild the broken motor? The first way is to consciously change your thinking. Be very aware of your thought processes. When self-defeating and guilt-inducing thoughts enter your mind, replace them with positive affirmations. Don't get trapped by the roadblock a lot of people run into, which is the belief that letting go and moving forward with life means they did not love the person they lost. This is definitely not true! The amount of love you have for someone does not equal the amount of time you have to grieve!

It definitely does not equal the amount of time you choose to punish yourself for not doing more.

As humans, it's our nature to form close bonds and develop loving relationships with significant attachments. If we never allow ourselves to move on after the loss of a loved one, then all our lives would be over as a result of losing someone we love. Whether or not you regain your happiness and zest for life doesn't depend on how much you loved the person, but it will depend on whether you remain parked in a negative, irrational belief system of guilt that keeps you from moving forward with your own life.

Moving forward and enjoying life doesn't mean you didn't love the person you lost. It simply means you have emotionally relocated them to a place where you can live the life you have been blessed with and can now celebrate the life they had. It is perfectly okay to let go of unhealthy beliefs and begin living life again after loss. Allow your loss to fuel you to live your life to the fullest. Take some time to reflect on your own beliefs about moving on after loss. If this is something you struggle with, it may help to write down your thoughts about moving on with your life and then replace these statements and thoughts with healthier and more positive affirmations.

Here is a suggestion for a possible way to turn around unrealistic thoughts of guilt over being happy and living your life. You could say, "Reinvesting in my own life does not mean that I did not love the person I lost, it means that I have grieved successfully and am ready to live the life I have been given."

Many people who are grieving—or are afraid to grieve—often say, "I just can't get over it." This statement automatically sets the tone for failure because to "get over something" symbolizes erasing memories and discontinuing any recollections of something or someone. This doesn't happen unless you have some sort of traumatic brain injury that has affected your memory. We will always have memories of our loved ones. Those memories are not going to simply erase or evaporate from our minds. However, we can get through the emotional pain that loss causes. By reframing "get over" to "get through," you set yourself up for a healthy grieving process that is attainable. You can't drive over other cars in a traffic jam to reach your destination. You get through traffic by changing lanes or taking some sort of action to move forward. So, you don't "get over" loss, you "get through" it with the appropriate process of grieving. By choosing to get through the traffic, you put yourself on the path to personal freedom.

FAILED RELATIONSHIPS

When we form close relationships with others, we build emotional connections and attachments that influence how we view ourselves and the world. These relationships could be with your parents, siblings or other family members, intimate partners, friends, etc. Secure attachments yield positive self-esteem and trust. Unsecure, troubled, or abusive relationships often yield lack of trust, self-doubt, isolation, mental and physical connection barriers, anxiety, fear, and loneliness. Oftentimes, people build up walls inside themselves as a means of protection from hurt because this may be all they've ever experienced in relationships. This, then, causes the erroneous belief that *everyone* they encounter will hurt them, too.

Every behavior, whether rational or not, serves some sort of purpose. The walls that people put up to protect themselves from the potential of being hurt also serve to keep love and fulfillment out. So, along with that perceived protection develops a barrier to healthy, satisfying relationships that we all need.

Humans have an innate need to love and be loved. Building walls to protect yourself is self-sabotaging and creates the very thing you may fear most—being alone. This is a perfect example of how people often create the very things they fear. By steering your attention to what you are afraid will happen or to what you don't want, you attract the worst-case scenarios created in your mind. By keeping others "out," you are also keeping out love and happiness.

Take a moment to think about some of the ways you may be potentially creating the circumstances you fear. If your biggest fear is that someone will hurt you and you will be all alone but you are already living this way by what you believe, what, then, do you have to lose by investing in new relationships? The worst-case scenario would be that you *would* get hurt and you would be alone, right?

Another factor to consider is that we get what we look for and expect in life. If you expect everyone to treat you badly, they probably will, or you will find something to reinforce this belief. Start expecting goodness! Start seeing this in yourself and in others! Envision the relationships you want, and allow yourself to fully immerse your being in the feeling of attaining them. By doing so, you program your Global Positioning System (GPS) for the right direction. But remember to be careful what you look for because you are certain to find it!

Examine the extent to which past relationships currently affect your life. Even though you may no longer be in contact with people who have hurt you, they may still control your every decision when it comes to formulating relationships with others and thus limit your happiness and joy. This is where it is absolutely essential that you put your foot down to the negativity you have experienced in the past in order to accelerate toward new, meaningful, and positive relationships with others. Start today by refusing to allow others' mistakes to control you, steering you toward a life of loneliness and depression. If you are angry, get angry enough to refuse to let them have control over you another day!

You see, it's easy to continue looking at life through the rearview mirror, missing the scenery ahead and focusing only on what is behind you. What would happen if you drove your car this way—looking only through the rearview mirror as you try to move forward? You are bound to make a wreck of it! In reality, we glance in the rearview mirror occasionally and use this to help us be aware of our surroundings and the obstacles that may be coming upon us for which we may need to stop, accelerate, or change lanes. Learn to use the past only as a guide, not a roadblock. Begin cleaning out the past from your trunk and stop staring in the rearview mirror so you can move forward toward relationships you deserve and desire.

ANGER

Perhaps you perceive yourself to be the victim of someone else's poor choices, and you are having trouble letting go of the anger and pain created from those experiences. While unfortunate, it's not uncommon for people to spend their entire lives full of anger and blame toward those who have done them wrong.

Hurt is a natural human reaction, but being a victim is a choice. People often believe that if they continue to hold on to anger it somehow "punishes" the other person and makes them the victim. However, the only person being punished is *you!* It's like taking poison and hoping it kills your enemy!

As long as you continue to hold on to anger, you become a victim of your own self and, therefore, the passive passenger in your own car! Despite the fact that the person(s) who hurt you may not be in your life now, holding on to the anger of your experiences is like having them in your presence and allowing them to harm you emotionally every day. The reality of the situation is that *you* are creating the pain and hurt for yourself! But the good news is that *you* can *choose* to stop this at any point! You can move from being the victim to being victorious!

If you are holding on to anger and, perhaps, blaming others for your unhappiness, lack of success, or lack of trust, the good news is there is hope! You can begin by acknowledging you have continued to travel down "Anger Road" day after day, month after month, and year after year—and have been getting extremely poor gas mileage! This means to acknowledge the reality of what is happening. Take ownership of what you are doing that fuels your anger.

You must assess how clenching the steering wheel of anger has served you all this time. Has it created peace or anxiety in your life? Has it improved your relationships and ability to trust others, or has it caused you to stay on back roads away from other cars? Has it allowed you to drive freely in the directions you desire to go, or has it kept your gearshift in park? Has it helped you shine, or has it caused your light to go dim?

If you recognize and admit that holding on to anger is not working for you, it is crucial to loosen your grip and apply the energy you have spent being angry toward changing your life direction. By changing direction, you're not admitting that what someone else did to you is okay, you are simply vowing to yourself that you will no longer travel down "Anger Road" where you know an accident is bound to happen.

Once you loosen your grip on anger, you are free to turn the wheel toward more positive life experiences. You become the driver who holds the key to your "inner state" of freedom, happiness, and control. If you want to be angry, then get angry enough to put your foot down to the fact that you are *no longer* going to let anyone be in the driver's seat of your life! No one can drive your car if you don't give them the keys! Choose to be the *victor* instead of the *victim,* and by doing so your life will take a detour in the right direction. Take back your keys, and go where you want to go in life peacefully and with a full tank of supreme fuel. Regardless of what has happened to you, you are still a supreme being!

PAST FAILURES

Maybe you have negative views of yourself stored away because of past learning experiences you have deemed as failures, and this has kept you from pursuing anything remotely associated with that experience. It is very important to distinguish between failing *at* something and *being* a failure.

For example, failing a test does not make you a failure. In order to succeed, you have to learn to accept that things do not always go as planned. Mostly, this "failure" is a blessing in disguise, and we very often give up before we find out what that "failure" was leading us to accomplish. The most important aspect to focus on is not the notion of "failing," but using what you have learned as fuel to move forward. Just because you may have taken one wrong turn, doesn't mean you turn the car around and drive home. Sometimes we must make a few "wrong turns" to get to where we are going. These "wrong turns" provide us with terrific scenery, insight, and perspectives we wouldn't have experienced on our one-way street. Can you think of times when things didn't go as planned but in the end turned out being better than you imagined? Our ability to bounce back from these wrong turns or unexpected detours is what programs us to succeed in life and gives us the ability to handle whatever life may throw at us. They are there to teach us how to employ our personal power during tough times.

Resiliency is one of the biggest predictors of success. Resiliency is the ability to move forward when bad things happen. It's the ability to see how good things *can* be as opposed to the way they are now. When you can learn to use your negative experiences to work toward a greater good, you have mastered a skill that will lay the groundwork for success. It's like putting a new frame on a picture—it makes a big difference how it looks, but it's still the same picture. Or stated another way, it's like putting fancy new rims on your car—it looks better, but it's still the same make and model and has the same engine and horsepower.

Have you ever observed two people experience the same event or circumstance but react totally different emotionally and behaviorally? The emotional response is a direct result of how each person decides to think about the situation. The emotional response then leads to our actions.

For example, Joe and Mark both received a speeding ticket on the way to work this morning. Joe was completely upset, cursing the officer who gave him the ticket and stayed red-faced and stressed all day at work. He lashed out at others and spent the day blaming the officer for "getting him." On the other hand, Mark, despite being disappointed about the ticket, comes to work making a joke about the ticket. He accepts full responsibility for speeding and states that this ticket probably saved his life today. Both individuals experienced the same stressor, but both chose to think about it and react in two different ways.

We have a choice of how we view the events in our lives, and we choose our reactions to those events. We can't always control everything that happens, but we have 100 percent control over how we react and deal with them. Therefore, nothing is going to happen to you in life that you can't handle. It is all a matter of mind-set.

You may be reading this and saying, "Yeah, right." Well, let me ask you this—what has happened in your life that you haven't made it through? The answer is *nothing!* If you are reading this book, there is nothing that has ever happened to you that you have not managed to make it through. You may feel broken, but you still persevered. When you focus your thoughts on this statement—that nothing is going to happen to you that you can't make it through—you lay the foundation for success and decelerate the fear that has held you back from living.

You could also choose an even higher road and say to yourself that there is nothing that is going to happen to you that you cannot use to help you thrive! You choose your attitude just like you choose your car. If you have deflated thinking and a bad attitude, you have a poor foundation for success. If you could picture this in terms of a vehicle, it would have dents, a cracked windshield, poor wipers, bad brakes, no gas, flat tires, a dead battery, and lost keys. Get the picture? Envision *yourself* as a vehicle. What would you look like? Sound like? Feel like? What is keeping you from accelerating to your full potential?

Whatever the case may be, examine what is stored in your "trunk." Make note of specific things that have been said and/ or done to you that you've not been able to let go of and that you believe have kept you from pursuing your dreams. Make a list of whatever you believe has kept you a passive passenger in your own car—whether it's words, past or current relationships, loss, past failures, or something else. When these obstacles are identified, challenged, and replaced with more realistic perspectives, you begin the process of scooting into the driver's seat and taking control of your life's journey. *You*, then, begin deciding your direction, not someone else! When you consciously decide to take control of your thoughts and beliefs, you put yourself on the path to empowerment. When you feel empowered, it is much easier to steer your way through adversity. Focus forward to the way you want your life to be instead of the way it has been. The more you focus on the negatives, the more negativity you will experience. By choosing to steer directly toward the positive, victorious version of yourself, you will attract more positive life experiences and greater feelings of fulfillment on your road to success.

Now that you have an awareness of the types of things stored in your trunk that weigh you down and halt your ability to move forward, let's talk about the items that *should* be stored in your trunk and travel with you everywhere you go— those things that help you out when you feel you are about to break down or run out of gas. These items will not only pre-vent catastrophic occurrences but will be very helpful in times of great need.

JUMPER CABLES

It can happen to the best of us when we least expect it. We get into our car and turn the key, but nothing happens. Our car won't start due to a dead battery. This usually happens unexpectedly and without warning. Distress has set in, and we are completely drained.

While stress is a normal part of life, we can let it take over to the point we are completely overwhelmed and exhausted, and if it continues, extreme and prolonged stress can lead to serious illness. When we let the stressors of life build up with-out utilizing positive coping skills and self-care, we experience a complete loss of energy and an inability to "start" again. Our batteries are drained!

While we are going about our daily lives traveling from one task to another, we fuel ourselves with the erroneous belief that we are doing something heroic by not taking time to take care of ourselves, and somehow this provides us with better gas mileage. In reality, we are *disempowering* and preventing our-selves from sustaining the energy needed to put the pedal to the metal and get where we want to go.

Every driver should carry a set of jumper cables in their trunk for those times when they need a boost. Not only are jumper cables a great item to have for our own use, but they could come in handy in assisting other drivers with drained or dead batteries. An important "road rule" to remember about jumper cables is that they require a positive battery to draw strength from and will not recharge if they are connected to another drained battery! Thus, if you feel your battery is drained, you cannot expect to gain strength from negative, pessimistic drivers whose batteries are already zapped. There is nothing more counterproductive than two drained batteries trying to get somewhere. I would bet at this moment you are envisioning battery drainers, right? It's good to gain perspective and clarity on those individuals who may be depleting you of energy and enthusiasm so you can make adjustments to your counterparts.

Perhaps another point to consider is how draining you are to other people's batteries. Positive people do not desire to spin their wheels with battery drainers. Have you heard the saying, "misery loves company"? Another point to consider is, even when your battery is fully charged, spending too much time with negative people will surely begin to drain it. So, it's necessary to remove yourself from battery drainers in order to be emotionally healthy and achieve success. This is difficult when the people who are draining the life out of you are family members or a significant other. Unfortunately, many people choose to remain in neutral instead of making the difficult decision to let go of these relationships.

It's okay to let go! You are ultimately responsible for your emotional health, energy, well-being, and establishing a strong foundation for the success you desire. If you allow others to drive you to the point of being emotionally drained and out of fuel, you will stay stuck. While the decision to let go of people, places, and things that drain your battery is tough, having a drained battery on the road of life is much tougher.

Surrounding yourself with positive people and utilizing your own positive affirmations will help to ensure that your battery stays charged with plenty of energy to go forward. Remember, dead batteries are one of the biggest reasons motorists find themselves on the sidelines!

POSITIVE SELF-AFFIRMATIONS

Positive self-affirmations are all the good things you can say to yourself that encourage and motivate you to accelerate in the direction of your goals and give you the "boost" you need. Make a list of all the positive things you can think of about yourself and all the things you would like to achieve. Some examples of positive affirmations include, "I can do it!" "I am capable!" "I deserve success!" "I have a lot to offer the world!" "I control my own direction!" "It is okay for me to invest in my own life!" "It's okay to move on with my life!" and "I deserve to be happy!" It's not only necessary, but it's crucial that these affirmations be stored where they are readily accessible on a moment's notice and applied often. Positive affirmations will be the weapon you use against negative, self-defeating thoughts and part of the path to achieving peace of mind and success. If you find yourself decelerating into a pattern of negative thoughts, replace them immediately with the positive ones you have available.

You may have ten negative thoughts before you become aware of them, but at that point, do not make it eleven. You wouldn't leave your car stuck in a ditch, would you? You wouldn't count the car a total loss simply because it's stuck and leave yourself without a car, right? Absolutely not! You'd take whatever action is necessary to get it unstuck. Well, it works the same way with our thoughts. Positive affirmations will keep you going in the right direction, free you when you detour toward negative thought patterns, and create feelings of confidence and assurance on your journey. Just as a car is a vessel to get you from point A to point B, your thoughts and positive self-affirmations are the vessels that will take you there as well. If you feel you are losing your personal power, examine your thoughts for they are the culprit of your emotions.

POSITIVE ATTITUDE

Perhaps the surest way to gain personal power in life is to maintain a positive attitude. A positive attitude should also be carried with you everywhere you travel in life. The one thing that we have complete control over is our thoughts and our attitude. We always have the power to choose our thoughts, regardless of the situation. We do not have control over someone being rude to us or unexpected detours. It's important to note that the storms of life may change our plans, but they do not have to ruin our lives. By adopting an overall positive attitude, you'll begin to see rainbows instead of rain, opportunities within obstacles, and divine guidance from temporary defeat. We may not have control over being stranded beside the road due to a snowstorm that hit unexpectedly, but we can control what we carry with us to help us weather the storm. We cannot control others' actions, or lack thereof, but we do have complete control over how we react to them.

Keeping a positive attitude will not only impact everything you set out to do but will make a grand difference in the enjoyment of the simplest of events in our daily lives. A positive attitude attracts positive people to you. Such an attitude is like having a clean, shiny car that's well maintained. Others are likely to notice it, appreciate its appearance, and be drawn to it. *You* are going to appreciate the way you feel as a result of having a positive attitude, too. In a sense, each day you are promoting yourself to others. The way you present yourself goes a long way toward attaining the things and relationships you want. More importantly, you are traveling through life with yourself and maintaining a positive attitude will make you a great companion on your journey.

Think about this—you'd have a hard time selling your car if it had a cracked windshield, flat tires, scratches, dents, and smoke coming from the exhaust. Perhaps, you may not even be able to give it away! Most likely, people will run in the opposite direction—away from the car—unless this is your goal. By maintaining a positive attitude, you set yourself up for success in both the outward things you desire and the internal feelings that are present with you each day of your life. A positive mental attitude is like having a car with a V8 engine. You're going to get where you want to go a lot faster with a lot more pizzazz and zest for life. Let this be empowering to you as you realize you have the "horsepower" needed to successfully handle any event or circumstance you encounter in life—*found in your attitude!*

SHOVEL

During the winter months when the weather gets cold and snowy, it's not uncommon for people to become stuck, spinning their tires in snow. This also happens when the people around us become "cold" and start to really come down on us. Before we know it, we're covered in the "coldness" of others and feel buried and stuck with little help to get back on our feet—or should I say, back into the driver's seat. This causes our self-esteem to suffer and stalls us from taking initiative to succeed. Sometimes, we are stalled there for long periods of time, while at other times we're able to shovel our way out. Digging out from bad weather is much more difficult if you do not have adequate tools.

Everyone should carry a shovel for the times they become stuck in "bad weather" and "coldness" from others. Having the right tools for the job of clearing a path for ourselves is exactly what we need to get back in the car and take the wheel. If you don't have adequate tools to get "unstuck," it's hard to say how long you'll remain stranded beside the road or, worse, in the ditch! For some, it's not until spring and the coming of warmer weather forces the snow to melt before they are able to move. For others, it's only the time it takes to grab the shovel and begin digging out of adversity despite the current conditions.

Think about your present situation and circumstances. Do you have the right tools to dig your way out? In what areas would a shovel be necessary to dig out of past experiences and clear the way for a better journey?

Simply having the shovel alone is not very effective. That's like having a car parked in the garage—you're not going anywhere. The real success comes from putting forth the effort and hard work necessary to dig yourself out of your current circumstances and negative past experiences. This is often where people tend to display avoidance, denial, and defeat. Sometimes people look at the work ahead of them and let themselves become defeated without even an attempt to dig themselves out. They just stand there, letting the "bad weather" overtake them.

When you receive others' coldness and then begin to repeat those cold, negative, and defeating words to yourself, you pour water on top of the snow and turn it into ice, making it even more difficult to get traction. Before you know it, you realize you've become the victim of an ice hole. The snowball effect then occurs. Negativity breeds more negativity, and before you realize it you've created an avalanche!

When you feel as if you're sitting on the curb watching others pass you by, it's easy to become angry and resentful. Those feelings get stored in your trunk and weigh you down. Those negative feelings influence every relationship you have and every interpersonal encounter. This is like driving down the road with mud all over your car. It affects how others see and interact with you as well as the way you perceive yourself. It becomes a vicious cycle.

To use the shovel effectively, you must first know what you need to dig out. The list of items in the first part of this chapter would be a great place to start because you must first identify the specific things that have caused you to be stuck. Sometimes we go through life avoiding the very things that enable us to move forward because we assume it will cause us pain to address them head-on. Just like the energy and hard work that goes into the physical shoveling of snow, it takes energy and hard work to address problems and work through them.

Consider that it can't be any harder than carrying dead weight around with you everywhere you go or than constantly falling victim to ice holes, right? At least after the hard work is over, you are free to accelerate toward your full power and potential. Do you have your shovel ready?

DUCT TAPE

It is recommended that drivers carry duct tape in their trunks in case they find themselves in a "sticky" situation. If we admit it, there have probably been many times that we wish someone would have duct-taped our mouths shut before we uttered some of the things we've said. On the other hand, there's probably been more times when you wish you had duct tape for someone else's mouth who just refused to put on the brakes!

If you truly want to be successful and viewed in a positive light, avoid gossiping and engaging in negative conversations about others. There is a quote by Eleanor Roosevelt that says, "Great minds discuss ideas; average minds discuss events; small minds discuss people."

You never know who could be walking by when you're talking negatively about others. This could be the person interviewing you for your dream job. It could be the person who has the potential to help you succeed. It could be the person you are set up with for a blind date! When the person you are having the conversation with walks away, they are going to wonder if you discuss them the way you were discussing someone else. This does not reflect positively on you and can come back to rear-end you someday.

Not only should you steer clear of negative talk about others because of the way they are likely to perceive you, but you should also swerve away from saying negative things to yourself because of the way *you* will perceive yourself. The conversation you have with yourself will either fuel you forward or disempower you. If you hold on to negative perceptions of yourself, you're likely to stay stuck—not in the passenger side of your car, but in the backseat on a dead-end street!

You must believe you can drive before you will ever have the courage to get behind the wheel. From this point forward, pay close attention to your self-talk. Every thought is programming your GPS, so make sure it's directing you on the right road. If you catch yourself saying demeaning and defeating things to and about yourself, bring out the duct tape, and put it to good use! Stick to positive self-talk instead!

Turn on your high beams and take the high road. Once you start carrying around duct tape, you'll be surprised at all it can do for you—*and others!* You will not regret it, and it will keep you out of a lot of sticky situations!

ANTIFREEZE

If you want to guarantee you'll not "freeze" at the most inopportune time, carry antifreeze in your trunk. This will prevent you from "freezing" with fear and will assist you in taking the appropriate actions toward success. Antifreeze can help you steer outside of your comfort zone to a new direction. How many times have you let fear stop you in your tracks? How many times has fear caused you to detour from a promising opportunity? How many times has fear kept you from committing yourself to a relationship?

Fear can paralyze you. It locks your gearshift in park. Fear robs you of your self-esteem and prevents you from finding and gripping the wheel of opportunities that cross over into your lane. Ask yourself if fear is the only reason you will not move forward with your ideas and plans. If the answer is yes— *go for it!*

Antifreeze is a key ingredient in your recipe for success, and the ingredients are quite simple—positive self-talk, belief in yourself, personal initiative, faith, action, and persistence. Take the wheel, or take the backseat!

Now you have a clearer picture of not only the items stored in your trunk that have kept you from moving forward, but you also have a better idea of what you *should* place in your trunk to ensure a pleasant journey and safe arrival. Cleaning out your trunk may be a difficult process, but you'll feel such freedom in letting go of those unnecessary items that weigh you down. When you remove the things that weigh you down and replace them with items that aid in getting you through adversity, you retain your personal power.

CHECKPOINTS

1. Identify items stored in your trunk that are preventing you from moving forward.

2. Drive straight toward them and address them head-on. Remove items that are no longer serving you in a positive manner. Replace with items that will increase your personal power—jumper cables, positive affirmations, positive attitude, shovel, duct tape, and antifreeze.

3. Surround yourself with positive energy—let go of battery drainers.

4. Steer your attention toward what you desire as opposed to the negative "what if" scenarios your mind creates.

5. By keeping others "out," you are also keeping out love and happiness.

6. Choose to accelerate toward the life you desire with your newfound freedom and personal power.

Use the Right Fuel

The type of fuel you use determines how smooth and efficient your car runs and directly impacts your drivability. In life, what you fuel yourself with directly influences health, emotional well-being, success, and overall physical and mental functioning. There are several different types of fuel we'll examine in this chapter in order for you to gain awareness and insight into the driving forces of your life. The first, and the most prominent, is your thoughts.

THOUGHTS AND SELF-TALK

What kind of fuel are you pumping into the car that takes you everywhere you need to go in life? In other words, what types of thoughts are most prominent for you—negative or positive? Self-affirming or self-defeating?

Your thoughts are like fuel for your car—if they are positive, they will drive you to success; if they are negative, they are more likely to steer you toward failure. Everything begins with a simple thought! Your thoughts create your feelings and, then, your actions and behaviors. Your thoughts cause you to push the gas pedal or the brakes. They either accelerate you or stop you from achieving your goals. Even though our thoughts are the one thing in life we have complete control over, thoughts seem to be one of the hardest things to master for many people.

We all have a choice regarding which fuel we'll use when we drive up to the gas pumps. We decide whether we want *diesel, regular, premium, or supreme.* Another factor that goes into our decision is the cost of that fuel. As of today, start thinking of the "cost" of your thoughts and beliefs and how they're determining your direction—or lack of direction—in your life. Negative thought patterns can cost you your job, healthy relationships, your health, your happiness, your peace of mind, and diminish your overall success. Your thoughts can cause you to miss opportunities that have been waiting for you, and when you don't achieve your desires you validate the negative, self-defeating beliefs you had from the beginning. Thoughts act as self-fulfilling prophecies. If you think you can, you will. If you think you can't, you won't.

Have you ever put diesel fuel into a gasoline tank? Hopefully not, but if you have, it probably wasn't a pleasant experience. Gasoline engines are not meant to run on diesel fuel, just as we are not meant to run on negativity. It is counterproductive. If you accidentally put diesel fuel into a gasoline engine, let me tell you what will occur—most likely, the gasoline engine will not run at all. The diesel fuel is likely to clog the fuel lines, fuel filters, and fuel injectors. If, by chance, the engine *does* run, it will give very poor performance.

The vast difference between a gasoline engine and a diesel engine is that the cylinders in a gas engine do not produce the same temperatures and pressures as those in a diesel engine. Diesel fuel will not ignite properly in a gasoline engine and can damage the gasoline engine's timing cycle and cylinder linings.

Now, you probably haven't done this with your actual gasoline engine, but have you used diesel fuel instead of the necessary gasoline in the form of your thoughts? I would be willing to bet that we all have done this before—many of us on a daily basis!

Negative thoughts can creep in without us realizing they're there. In other words, they can creep in by accident. However, the more "accidental" negative thoughts one has, the more they become habit. These self-defeating thoughts become beliefs, which contribute to your self-concept. Your self-concept determines the types of goals you'll set for your life and the amount of effort you'll put in to achieving them. Negative thoughts will continue until you become aware of them and choose to change them. We must confront, challenge, and replace negative thinking in order to accelerate and stop spinning our wheels in a cycle of negativity. We cannot change anything until we become aware of it. Once we *are* aware, we have full power to take control of our own thoughts, feelings, and behaviors and thus our direction.

Now, the simplest solution to fixing diesel fuel in a gasoline tank is to siphon the diesel fuel out of the gas tank and refill the tank with regular unleaded gasoline. The car should run even if there is some diesel remaining in the fuel mixture, but you can expect lower fuel mileage and more smoke in the exhaust until the diesel fuel is flushed from the system.

We can't expect to achieve our goals and dreams by attempting to operate on bad fuel. Even a small amount of bad fuel causes significant problems. Never underestimate the power of just one negative thought. Every day when you wake up, decide what type of fuel you'll use—this will dictate the quality of your day, your relationships, and your overall life satisfaction.

Aim for supreme thoughts—thoughts that motivate, reassure, increase confidence, and promote peace of mind. At the first sign of negativity, siphon it out and replace it with more positive, affirmative thoughts. The longer you allow negativity to persist, the more diesel you are pouring into your gasoline engine and the more damage you are creating. You can determine what type of fuel you're using by examining your mood and energy level. If you're weary, bogged down, depressed, and fearful, it's a sure sign your thinking needs to be adjusted. Remember, our feelings are a direct result of our thoughts, and you can use this mile marker to alert you to the location of your thoughts. Your thoughts either drive you crazy or drive you successful, and you have complete power over which path you choose.

The unfortunate fact is that most people cling to their negative thoughts and accept them as truth. They believe the lies they tell themselves and the lies others tell them as well. One negative comment from someone else seems to fuel people's actions—or lack of action. Why is it that we can receive ten compliments during the day but dwell on the single negative comment someone said to us when we lie down to go to sleep at night? Why does negativity seem so much more powerful at times? Why do we, as humans, tend to accentuate the negative and minimize the positive?

How do we stop this? We must make a conscious choice to refuse to let the negative control us, driving us away from where we want to go in life. We must consciously and carefully choose our thoughts and our focus and create a new pathway in our brain. If you are tired of driving down the same one-way street, now is the time to turn around. We must also consider the source from which the negative comment or action came. There are a variety of reasons people try to put you down or discourage you. Mostly, it comes from that person's own insecurity or jealousy. Instead of dwelling on the negative, learn to see these comments or gestures from others as a sign that you are on the right path to success! Don't let negativity consume you! Make it work for you as fuel to strive for greatness and to become the best person you can.

There was once a seventh-grade student who played flute in the school band. She practiced every day and had challenged the senior flute players for their seats. To be first chair was the highest position in each instrument section. The student won challenge after challenge and was seated first chair despite only being in seventh grade. As a result, she was picked on, had part of her uniform stolen before a big game, and the other students would throw things at her on the bus. Did she let this stop her from doing what she did best? Absolutely not! She used this as positive fuel to practice more and maintain her first-chair position! Another person may have given up and said that it was not worth it and diminished their own abilities due to others' actions. When you are good at something or you have a grand dream, never let anyone else keep you from success or from becoming all you can be. This story also provides a good example of how you must consider the source. It was probably demeaning to the seniors who lost their seats to a seventh grader, and their jealousy caused them to react negatively to the obviously very talented flutist!

Other people's comments do not define you! You are the only one who has the power to do that! If you are driving a Mazda, the simple fact that someone doesn't like it does not change the brand name or its popularity and success. You are your own brand, make, and model, and no one has the power to change who you truly are!

Understand that anytime you are doing great things and are on the road to success, you can expect to run into negativity and opposition from time to time—anticipate it, use it as positive fuel when it occurs, release it from controlling your destination, and keep moving forward. When you come to a bump in the road, you don't pull over and park. You get around it and keep going. What would happen if every car stopped when they came to a small bump in the road? There would likely be traffic jams, accidents, angry people, and no one would get where they were going.

FOOD

Another form of fuel that directly impacts your performance is the food you eat. Food is fuel for the body and mind. Food directly influences the way you think, feel, and behave. Have you ever eaten a certain food and become lethargic or had difficulty thinking or functioning a while afterward? The statement "you are what you eat" could not be more accurate! What you put into your body will directly influence your performance, just as the type of fuel you use in your automobile affects its performance.

It's also important to examine the cost of what you're eating. Many people state they can't afford to eat healthy or they don't have time to cook healthy meals. In response, if you fill your body with junk that diminishes your health and ability to function optimally, you'd better start planning to have time to be sick!

Eating healthy is an investment in yourself and those who love and depend on you. Just as an automobile will not get you where you want to go if it is running on bad fuel, your body and mind will not be able to lead you to success if you are feeding them unhealthy things. Eventually, you are going to stall out and lose your drive!

SUBSTANCES

Many people drive through life intentionally avoiding what is visible in their rearview mirror, the negative items stored in their trunk, or events and circumstances going on around them. All too often, people turn to chemical substances in an attempt to deal with painful memories and negative feelings they've experienced. These people end up driving through life completely "gassed" with inhibited visibility, drivability, and success-ability.

When you travel on your life's journey, drive under positive influence. Surround yourself with positive people who have vision and fearless acceleration toward their goals. Align with those people who encourage you to strive for your full potential and who help you accelerate in the right direction at full speed. Seek out books, people, speakers, movies, videos, etc. that inspire you to be the best make and model of yourself you can be. Strive to be a person *of* substance—not dependent on a substance.

SELF-CARE

As discussed earlier, if you put the wrong type of fuel in your car, it's not going to run well or may need a complete overhaul. Are you in need of an overhaul? Have you been running on "bad fuel"? Remember, your thoughts are your fuel! Make the choice today to begin running on positive, self-affirming thoughts rather than negative, self-defeating thoughts. Perhaps the most important thing we can do for ourselves, as well as others, is engage in self-care. Just as your car could not continue to run on bad fuel or flat tires, you will not be able to continue to function without investing in your own self-maintenance.

Some people have the mistaken belief that investing in their own self-care is selfish and that they should devote all of their time to others instead. This would be like making sure all the other vehicles on the road have good fuel, inflated tires, and oil changes but never spending a moment maintaining your own vehicle. It simply doesn't work! If you're not investing in your own self-care, you too will attempt to run on empty but will be forced to pull over beside the road, leaving you unable to get to those who need you. You then become a bystander on the road of your own life, unable to assist any other drivers in need and watching time and opportunities pass by you.

Take care of yourself! Your body is the vessel that gets you from point A to point B! It must be well taken care of to operate smoothly and to make it where it needs to go in life. Your level of self-care will equal your drivability. Many people's roads are cut short and become dead ends due to lack of self-care. Take some time to do things that you enjoy! Things that bring you happiness, joy, peace, and serenity! Make *yourself* a priority. You are important and must treat yourself as such. You are in the driver's seat here!

GRATITUDE

Gratitude is perhaps one of the most optimal forms of fuel you can run on. By shining your headlights on the things you are grateful for, you will begin to see a significant increase in life experiences that bring you deep appreciation. By shifting your focus to that of appreciation, you immediately begin to increase your energy and vibration. The more good-feeling thoughts you choose, the better you will feel! What if tomorrow you lost everything that you didn't acknowledge gratitude for today? What would you be left with? This question really puts things in perspective. While you're busy being distracted by negative things lying along the roadway, you lose sight of the beautiful things that surround you.

What you repetitively focus on becomes your life experience. Wouldn't you much rather experience the pleasure of deep appreciation for what exists in the present moment than worry about what isn't working or what you don't have? If you really want to increase your vibration, express gratitude in advance for things that have not yet occurred as if you know it is a done deal. Expressing thanks for a safe arrival at your destination, even though you just pulled out of the driveway, is a prime example of gratitude in advance. Trusting the journey can be difficult, especially if you cannot see the final stretch of roadway. By practicing gratitude for what is now and what will be, you pave the way for successful travels.

What are you grateful for today? Your family? Friends? Health? Running water? Money in the bank? Food in the fridge? It's amazing how much we take for granted on a daily basis. We tend to get in our cars, drive down the road—most of the time focused on what we have to do, dreading where we are going, regretful of where we've been, and replaying the bumps in the road we've experienced. We sometimes take for granted the fact that there's gas in our car, the headlights work, the transmission is operating well, the brakes work, etc. I challenge you to take at least a few moments each day to focus on what you are grateful for in your life. You will amaze yourself at how many wonderful things are present in your life that await to be acknowledged. The more you acknowledge, the more you'll see.

To really accelerate your ability to transform adversity into fuel for your journey to success, learn to express gratitude for the bumps in the road and the unexpected detours. Trust you are being guided in the right direction and that everything is working out in your favor, even if you don't understand it right now. Sometimes what appear to be the biggest failures and disappointments are the biggest blessings in disguise! Even if you are at your lowest point right now, you are being prepared and polished for your destiny! When you experience negative situations, failures, disappointments, or criticism from others, step outside the context of those experiences and examine what life is trying to teach you. Adapt the belief that the universe is working in your favor, never against you. Henry Ford stated, "When everything seems to be going against you, remember that the airplane takes off against the wind, not with it."

Once you step out of the emotional aspect of these experiences, you gain more objective awareness into how these things are being used to help you grow and develop into the person you are meant to be. You realize you are not a failure but a student in training, much like a car being sanded and prepared for new paint. If you hear a noise coming from your car and can't figure out where it's coming from, get out of the car and observe closely. Removing yourself from the car will give you a clearer perspective on what's really going on. Step out of your own thoughts and simply observe what your mind is thinking. Separating yourself from your thoughts can help provide a clearer perspective. Becoming the observer of your thoughts also empowers you to realize that you are so much more than what you think.

Trust you are being navigated in the right direction, and refuse to let your journey end in defeat! Trust you are being polished and the end result is beautiful! Embrace difficulties with appreciation of what they are preparing you to experience. True growth and transformation requires the ability to be truly thankful for your perceived enemies and difficult life experiences, for these all helped develop a higher version of you that you would not have attained otherwise. It is solely up to you to syphon those experiences into high-grade fuel for your journey. Let adversity "fuel" you, not "fool" you.

CHECKPOINTS

1. Determine the type of fuel you are using in your daily drive with life.

2. Siphon out the bad fuel and replace with supreme fuel in the form of your thoughts.

3. Increase your self-care to make your ride smoother and more enjoyable.

4. Take time to express gratitude every day, even for the things you have not seen.

5. Others' opinions do not define you—refuse to give away your power.

GIVE YOURSELF A TUNE-UP

Your car's engine is made up of numerous components working together to ensure that your vehicle starts and runs properly. Over time, these components can wear out, resulting in loss of performance. Sometimes your car may seem to be running fine, and you put off getting a tune-up thinking everything is okay. Sometimes symptoms are subtle and hard to recognize until they are to the point of disabling your car. You know you are in need of a tune-up if you are experiencing a decrease in gas mileage, loss of power, or your engine is knocking, hard to start, stalling, or stopping. It is important to listen and observe what is really going on within you instead of overlooking or ignoring the nudges you encounter along your journey.

Negative self-talk, feeling bad about yourself, constantly comparing yourself to others, fear of stepping out of your comfort zone or of what could go wrong, being stagnant or depressed or anxious are all signs that you're in need of a mental tune-up. If you want a successful journey and the assurance that you can travel through life without breaking down, it's crucial that you identify and take immediate action to remedy any identifiable problems *before* they spin recklessly out of control. Let's take a look underneath the hood to see if you are experiencing any of the following signs of a needed tune-up.

ENGINE WON'T START

This is one of the most common types of car trouble and is usually due to unperformed maintenance. In this case, we will say unperformed maintenance of your mind. Do you ever have trouble getting started on a task or project? Maybe it's exercising, daily tasks, chores, or taking steps to achieve your goals? Sometimes we have goals we want to accomplish and dreams we want to come true, but we just cannot seem to find the motivation to begin. Maybe the journey seems too long, and we choose to stay parked safe in our driveway. But staying in park can lead to feelings of failure and regret. Unfortunately, people allow their lack of progress to be a direct reflection of their abilities and intelligence. This is not an accurate representation of one's capability or intelligence, but rather a direct representation of faulty thinking. Faulty thinking creates the behaviors that prevent successful completion of goals.

The next time you have trouble getting started, take a look underneath your hood. Examine what you are telling yourself about your journey, how you feel when you think these thoughts, and whether or not your thoughts are fueling you with fear or confidence. Once you're able to pinpoint how you're pulling the brake on true potential, you're ready to replace the parts that are no longer working in your favor.

Think of one thing you want to do, but you haven't moved forward with. What is it? What are your thoughts about this particular desire? Write them down, and reflect on how your thoughts have contributed to your inability to start. There's a direct correlation between thoughts and behaviors. Once you've identified defeating thoughts, write a new list of reassuring thoughts and affirmations. This will help get you started moving in the right direction. This is the only head-on collision you would want to have happen. Until you face your faulty thinking head-on, it will continue to disempower you and make you believe things about yourself that are not true.

You must also be aware of interference from others and how others' words or actions may be inhibiting you from starting. Others' words can be toxic to your success if you allow them to. Add people to your list of things you perceive as stalling your car. Perhaps even make a list of specific comments you've been told that keep replaying in your mind—like a bad song on the radio that makes you sick every time you hear it. Sometimes, it's necessary to remove or distance yourself from people who negatively affect your operating abilities. While this is often a tough decision to make, I promise it's much easier than a life of regrets of not living up to your full potential.

If you're engaging in regular maintenance and addressing issues as they arise, the likelihood of your engine refusing to start decreases. In other words, you maintain your personal power. By exhibiting personal initiative early on, your motivation and ability to keep moving increases and fuels you in the right direction. Taking personal initiative and having the courage to face issues head-on fuels you in a positive direction. You eliminate further burdens from getting stored in your trunk and holding you back from achieving the things you desire in life.

The good news is that, even if your engine is not starting now, you have the built-in power to rev it up and get started again with more power than ever before! All it takes is a conscious decision to not just idle through life, a personal initiative to get restarted, and a determination to keep on going.

ENGINE STARTS, BUT STOPS

Have you ever started out really motivated to accomplish something and then, after some time, your motivation diminishes and you do less and less to work toward your goals? What causes this deceleration? Perhaps you may feel that it's taking too long to achieve your goal, and instead of sticking it out you decide it's not worth continuing, so you quit. Sound familiar? All too often, people give up when they are so close to success. They stop believing in their dreams and in themselves. They stop believing they will ever reach their destination. They fuel themselves with thoughts of defeat and live their lives never knowing what they were truly capable of achieving. Are you one of these people?

Think about a small child who expresses his or her dream of becoming an astronaut, doctor, scientist, etc. If you've ever witnessed a child talk about what they want to be when they grow up, they tend to express this with such enthusiasm. Children seem to have no doubts that they will accomplish their heart's desire, and they tend to see the world as full of endless possibilities. Perhaps you were the child who expressed your dreams so vibrantly to others, and somewhere along the way you stopped talking about them. You stopped believing in your dream and yourself. What happened to change this excitement and eager expectation for your future? Can you pinpoint when this occurred? Reexamine the things stored in your trunk as these items can give insight into what stopped you from dreaming.

If you have a dream, don't ever give up on it no matter how difficult the road may be. You never know just how close you could be to making it a reality. The detours you are experiencing may be there to push you farther in the direction of your dream instead of away from it. Detours are not roadblocks. In order to achieve your desires, you have to believe you can achieve them. Anything is possible if you believe! When you find yourself losing speed, envision how your life will be once you achieve your dreams. Imagine every detail you can, and allow yourself to experience how good it feels to have accomplished your dreams. Your imagination and visualizations will help keep your engine running to drive you to success. They fuel your inner drive and increase your personal power to live the life you imagine. Take some time to regroup and refocus. If you take a wrong turn when driving, you don't just park—you take a moment to map out the best course of action to get back on the road.

ROUGH IDLE

Engine idle is said to be a good measure of your engine's health. If there are problems going on under the hood, there's a good chance they will affect your idle speed and quality. *Rough idle* can be defined as uneven or erratic engine idle, which may cause the engine to stall or the vehicle to shake. *Idle* can also be defined as not working or inactive, doing nothing, or having no basis or reason. Sometimes a rough idle can even make it seem like you are going to die.

How many times does the stress of life get you to the point where you think you cannot take anymore? Perhaps you think you are not going to survive whatever you're going through. Hang on to the wheel—the road may be bumpy, it may be foggy ahead, your lights might be dim, the rain may be pouring down, and your car may be about to run out of gas, but just keep going! If you let it, stress and faulty thinking can cause you to sputter through life and stall when it comes to accomplishing your dreams. Affirm to yourself that you are growing and doing great—even if you are struggling. If the butterfly did not have to struggle to break free from the cocoon, it would never learn to fly. The same is true for you. You are in the process of continued growth, and you must trust the process. In the end, you'll realize how resilient you really are.

Everyone fights their own battles, and the most common weapon we use to destroy and defeat ourselves is our thoughts. However, the good news is that as long as your car is idling, it is still running. Also, you are the only person who has the power to steer your thoughts in the direction you want. As long as you are still breathing, you still have the "drive" in you. You may be idling rough and you may be stalling at times, but you still have the potential to achieve anything you desire and arrive at any destination you choose. Stop allowing yourself to just idle through life. Every day holds so many potential positive experiences and opportunities, but you must keep your sense of drive and purpose.

Think about your reasons. Why do you want to achieve your dreams? Let your reasons program the GPS. Get specific on what you want and where you want to go. Take some time right now to reprogram your GPS. Don't worry about how long it will take you to get there, just think about how you will feel when you arrive. Make a point to enjoy each and every moment of your journey. Oftentimes, a programmed GPS will take you on the shortest route. This is not always the best drive. If you pass up a turn, don't worry—your GPS will reprogram and still get you there. After all, what you experience and who you become on your journey is the best part of the ride.

POOR ACCELERATION

Sometimes, we are highly motivated to begin our journey. We're like a V8 engine ready to go. We have our destination clear in our heads, but after some time we lose our ability to keep accelerating. It can become difficult to know which road to take or how you will achieve your goals. You may become discouraged because you don't know every single street you're going to take to get there.

It's important to start where you are and accept that you don't need to know every single detail in advance. Once you've made your desires known and you hold an unswerving belief that you'll get there, the universe will send people and opportunities your way when you need them. There will be people and opportunities you will encounter that you have no way of knowing about in advance. Take this pressure off yourself and start trusting that your journey is unfolding exactly the way it is supposed to unfold. Trust that the universe will guide and steer you in the right direction after you have driven off in complete faith.

By pushing the gas pedal, you start moving and you're not just idling. Even if you take an unexpected road, you are not lost or defeated. The most important thing is that you restart and keep accelerating. The more you continue to hold the visions of what you want in life, the faster you will get there. Unexpected roads may begin to appear to you after you begin your journey—roads you know you must take, but that were not in your original plan. These are likely to be roads you never thought were drivable.

By continuing to envision your destination and having faith that you'll definitely arrive, you'll attract the right people, places, and things to help guide you on your journey. Opportunities will find you, but you must stay alert at the wheel as you can miss important signs of the paths you need to take. You must keep a positive mind-set with the expectation that things are always working out for you. A negative mind-set will cloud opportunities.

Think about this. One small snowflake may seem insignificant on its own, but many joined together can create an avalanche. Unfortunately, this is what happens with our thoughts. One negative thought joined by several others can cause a 20-car pileup and mass destruction to your life. Use reverse to your advantage. One positive thought in the right direction joined by many other positive thoughts can accelerate you at speeds you never knew existed. The great news is there are no speeding tickets, only your ticket to success!

Keep accelerating, even if you are only going five miles an hour. If you accomplish just one small thing today in relation to your goal, today is a success. Even if what you accomplish seems miniscule, it is building your life one step by one step. You are getting closer to your goals. Now, sit back and give yourself some praise for even the smallest distance you have come in the right direction. You are well on your way, and everything is unfolding perfectly!

KNOCKING

Knocking noises from your engine can sometimes be caused by a tank of inferior gas, but it most definitely indicates that something more significant is going on that needs your attention. Do you ever hear knocking from underneath your hood? I mean, like there is something trying to tell you something. Something that is saying to you, "Is there anyone in there?" or "Let me in!" I am referring to the "real" you that exists beneath all the noise and clutter and interference from the outside world and the forces of your own mind. The "you" at your core that is a divine creation of endless possibilities. The little voice inside you that whispers ideas, dreams, and aspirations that the "false" you negates or dismisses out of fear of failure.

Have you ever had a thought about something you would like to do but talked yourself right out of it? Maybe you let self-doubt or fear steer you away, and you continue to ignore the knocking you're hearing. This is a sure sign of something you need to give your attention to.

What is the "real" you trying to say? What is your inner voice trying to steer you toward or away from? When you can figure out what's really going on, you can successfully tend to it so that you're sure to accelerate with good horsepower and drive while nurturing and promoting your authentic self.

POWER LOSS

It is said that a dirty filter is a common cause of power loss. One of the most self-destructive things we do to ourselves is give away our power to other people by not appropriately filtering their actions and comments through our own thought system. By power, I mean power over how smoothly you run in terms of your mood and sense of self-worth.

What comments from others have you allowed to pass through your filter and defeat you? What past failures have you allowed to steer you away from your true potential? Anytime you fail to appropriately filter toxins from your environment, you are sure to end up with clogged perceptions that will inhibit your success and well-being. Any negative emotional or behavioral reaction you have in response to others' negativity shifts your power and immediately hands the keys of your well-being to someone else. You are then driven mad or sad and away from what you want and the way you want to feel. You lose your sense of peace, and the road becomes full of potholes that destroy your alignment with your true self. You must filter *everything* so that whatever tends to decrease your personal power will remain outside your car—or, should I say, outside your focus. This is what enables your car to run with full horsepower and remain in alignment with who you really are.

When someone says something to you, ask yourself the following questions: "Will driving around with this comment serve my best interests?" "Does it motivate me?" "Does it make me feel good about myself?" "Does it accelerate me toward my goals?" If the answer to any of these questions is "no," filter it out of your mind and refuse to fuel yourself with such pollutants.

Whether your engine has refused to start or you have been hearing knocking from underneath your hood, you must realize that you cannot ignore all the signs that indicate you are in need of a tune-up. Tune-ups are crucial to your success and personal power, and you must stay awake and alert to your internal guidance system. It will tell you when you are not aligned with your potential and authentic self and will guide you in the right direction if you listen and follow it.

No one has power over you unless you give it to them. You can't control everything that happens in your environment, but you can control everything that happens in your mind. If someone pulls up beside you, revs their engine, and wants to race you, let them go. You have a V8 engine that could leave them in a cloud of dust, and you don't even have to push the gas pedal! The race is really within yourself. The problem lies not in what someone else says or does to you but in your reaction to it. Your thoughts about these events are what diminish your power or empower you. So, what are you going to do? Will you keep giving others power over you, or will you empower yourself with drive and determination?

No matter how good you are at driving through life, tune-ups are *always* needed. There is a big difference between a tune-up and an overhaul. Tune-ups are inevitable. Overhauls are only needed when you fail to conduct tune-ups. You must constantly identify areas of poor performance, make appropriate diagnoses, and repair as needed. Sometimes you must even replace parts that are no longer working. Never stop growing and stretching yourself. Don't be afraid of outgrowing those close to you, and refuse to let *anyone* hold you back. You can't neglect your own car because the one next to you is about to break down. You are always in a state of expansion and growth with unlimited possibilities. Tap into all your resources—both internal and external—and not only will you survive life's journey, but you'll truly enjoy every mile of it! You'll be able to recognize that even the detours and potholes are signs you are being guided by something much greater than yourself. Trust the process!

CHECKPOINTS

1. Pull over and listen to your inner voice. What is it telling you?

2. Identify areas of your life that are causing you to stall. Take immediate action before problems escalate out of control.

3. Realign your thinking and tune back to what you want. Envision having it all right now. Feel it, experience it, and express gratitude in the present moment.

4. Continue to assess for areas that need improvement and maintenance.

5. Filter out negativity in order to ensure your personal power.

6. As long as you are breathing, you still have the "drive" in you. You have the potential to achieve anything you desire.

Engage in Regular
Maintenance

Even the best cars will leave you stranded beside the road if they are not regularly maintained. You must engage in regular maintenance, or "self-care," if you expect to reach your goals and arrive at your desired destinations. Without regular maintenance, you'll end up sitting curbside on the road of life. Unless I'm terribly mistaken, you wouldn't be reading this book if you were willing to settle for a curbside life!

If you do find yourself settling, consider this your curbside assistance. Perhaps you've established dreams and goals for your life and you have a strong belief that you will achieve them, but you struggle with self-care. Maybe your lack of self-care has left you feeling depleted, worn, or burnt out. Many people hold on to the false belief that it's selfish to take care of themselves and that they should be focused on others only. Do you ever feel guilty for taking time for yourself—maybe to read a book, go to the gym, take a walk, or to simply just be?

Many people say they can't find the time to engage in self-care and that other things are more important on their to-do list. Lack of time and guilt are the biggest reasons people report not engaging in regular self-maintenance. The level of self-care you engage in is directly tied to your thoughts and beliefs. If you think of yourself as unworthy, incapable, or selfish, you are probably not engaging in the maintenance necessary to continue running smoothly. When you don't reach your desired destination, you allow your false beliefs of not being worthy or capable to be reinforced. On the other hand, if you recognize the need to take care of yourself so that you *can* offer the best version of you to the world, you're likely to be engaging in regular self-maintenance.

An entire car runs on the engine and fuel. You run on your thoughts, which start or stop your engine and either fuel you or cause you run out of gas. Let's examine specific items that need regular maintenance on a car in order to keep it running at its full capacity.

TIRES

Wear patterns on tires indicate aggressive driving, improper inflation, and worn suspension components. It's crucial to keep good tread on your tires if you want to travel safely. Lack of tread can lead to potentially dangerous driving conditions.

Are you tired of the same old roads you take day after day? Are you tired of sputtering through life and feeling deflated? Are you having trouble turning the curves of life without being spun around in the wrong direction? Now is the time to take charge! Get tired of being tired!

We become tired and unmotivated when our tires are unbalanced and not in proper alignment. Align your thoughts and feelings with what you want in life. If you don't turn the wheel in the direction you want to go, you'll end up somewhere else.

You know when you're not in alignment because the road is bumpy, your emotions become jarred, and you feel deflated and flat. Imagine trying to drive somewhere with four flat tires, or even one flat tire. Moving forward simply isn't going to happen. At this point, it doesn't matter how good the exterior condition of your car is, it's not going to be able to go anywhere.

There are four specific areas that lead to deflation—lack of clear vision for the future, lack of specific plans, lack of action, and lack of belief in one's self to achieve their desires. You must believe in yourself—even when no one else does. You must believe in yourself when other drivers cut you off, run you out of the road, or try to tell you you're going the wrong way. If you don't believe you can drive, you will never get behind the wheel. If you don't believe you will arrive, you will never get your gearshift out of park.

To ensure your tires have plenty of tread, rotate them regularly. Do things you don't normally do. Take some risks and step out of your comfort zone. Give yourself permission to create a healthy balance of work and play. Spend time doing things you love with the people you love. Spend time alone to reflect on your journey and where you are headed. Align yourself with people who inflate your happiness and well-being. Practicing all of these things will help prevent your tires from going flat.

Regularly check the air in your tires. When you discover one is low, fill it with any or all of these things. Replace your tires with new ones when the old ones have driven their course. Don't wait until you are stranded to do this.

LIGHTS

Headlights have come standard on vehicles for over a century. It's obvious why you would need them. There are times you can drive without your lights on and be fine, such as during the daytime hours, but headlights are desperately needed during downpours and in the darkness of night. But what happens if your lights are dim or burned out?

Picture yourself driving down the highway. It's a dark night. The road is curvy, and you can't see very far in front of you because your headlights are dim. You can't see what's ahead of you, and others are having a hard time seeing you, too. Consider the potential liability this situation could hold if someone doesn't see you or sees you too late. With dim headlights, you are hoping other drivers notice that your vehicle is also on the road. Your anxiety level is high because you don't know what lies ahead. Your frustration level is elevated due to the continuous struggle of getting where you want to go. You realize your fate is determined by whomever is driving in the other lane from you. A scary scenario, wouldn't you agree?

The headlights are the first thing another driver sees when you are driving at night. The other driver will steer their car according to what they see. If you do not "shine" in your chosen profession and rarely go the extra mile, you are likely to be passed for promotions. On the other hand, if you are "shining" in your profession, you may also meet with adversity from your colleagues who are uncomfortable with your success. You could be sideswiped by criticism and loss of relationships out of others' insecurity and jealousy. You will miss opportunities if you hold back from being who you really are. Don't let anyone steal your drive!

Our ability to illuminate ourselves comes standard with each of us as well, but each of us must choose to use a different type of light. As the person who holds the keys and drives the car, you have complete control over when you turn on the lights and how bright they shine.

The headlights of a car give the driver a clear picture of what lies ahead as well as serve as a beacon for other drivers to see you coming. They also serve as a tool to help get you to your destination and to indicate to others that you're there. Headlights prevent others from colliding with you on your journey. How far do you think you'll safely get on your journey with dim headlights? How will this affect your drivability?

In order to achieve success, we must shine light wherever we go. We have to be able to stand out and not just blend in with the scenery. This is how people often get passed up on their journey to success.

Successful people aren't without faults or weaknesses, but they are willing to shine light on their own shortcomings, pull themselves out of the dark, and address obstacles head-on. Successful people use daytime running lamps to look for any opportunity to improve and gain insight and self-awareness.

They are constantly seeking out new ideas and paths to a better road to self-discovery. Because life can throw anything in front of us at any time, it's crucial to be prepared to be alert to what's coming at you or to see your way clear through adversity when it's in front of us.

The simple fact that your headlights are dim doesn't mean you are hopeless and should pull over and junk your car. It means you have simply realized your dim lights need your attention. In order to brighten or adjust your headlights, you must examine the type of lights that you are currently utilizing. Do you use incandescent bulbs, halogen, xenon, driving lights, pencil beam, fog lights, or LEDs?

Incandescent Bulbs

Incandescent bulbs have been around for over a century and are considered one of the most common forms of headlights used by automakers. This bulb is described to work much in the same way as a lamp bulb but more powerfully. Incandescent bulbs shine out brilliantly and are characterized by ardent emotion and intensity.

Despite having more power than a lamp bulb, the filament used in these bulbs tends to evaporate over time and burn out. Are you an incandescent bulb? Well, most likely, you haven't been around over a century, but it's not uncommon for people to allow themselves to "evaporate" from truly living life and for burnout to set in.

Engaging in regular self-care will keep your bulbs shining bright. If something is causing you to feel burned out, replace the bulb and keep shining. Consider it necessary maintenance.

Find your passion again. Do small things that illuminate your inner self and put you into alignment with what you want and who you want to be. You are more powerful than you realize. You are a brilliant creation made to shine.

Halogen Bulbs

Halogen bulbs are similar to incandescent bulbs. However, there are two differences—the halogen bulb uses a thinner filament that offers a brighter white light, and the bulb is filled with halogen gas that extends the life of the filament. Are you more of a halogen bulb? What are you doing right now that will extend the quality of your life or length of life itself? Your input directly affects output. If you want to live a long, peaceful, healthy, successful life, you must engage in activities that promote what you desire.

Xenon Bulbs

Xenon bulbs have been growing in popularity due to their increased brightness. These bulbs are able to generate almost three times the illumination of the halogen bulb and can last ten times longer. Given this description, are you running on xenon bulbs? Who comes to your mind whom you would consider as using xenon bulbs? Is it someone with a lot of energy? Is it someone who leaves you feeling good after you've been around them?

Everything is made up of energy. People exhibit different energy vibrations, and it feels good to be around people with great energy. What type of maintenance do you need to do to make sure you put off good vibes? Who are you surrounding yourself with that dims your light? Who do you surround yourself with that helps you shine?

Maintain relationships that bring out the best in you. When you shine to your true potential, you'll attract others who shine as well. This is how you light up the world—not just the night.

Driving Lights

Driving lights go with you everywhere you travel in life. This is what other people see every day. Driving lights are standard on most vehicles today and usually have a high and low beam setting in order to adjust to different driving conditions. Sometimes you must adjust your shine to outside conditions. High beams are great, but you must guard against blinding other drivers. Spending too much time talking about yourself and not showing enough interest in others will deter others from interacting with you. It can cost you good opportunities as well. Be the light that drives others to succeed. This is the road that will lead you to your greatest success. Help other drivers when they are stranded or broken down. When you help others you are helping yourself. In life, you get back what you put out. Be a light to others, and don't be afraid to shine. Always remember that you get nowhere when you blind others from seeing your true potential.

Pencil Beams

These lights are long-range for up to 2,000 feet and have a narrow horizontal spread. In some states, these lights are not legal for street use; their brightness value and mounting location can often blind other drivers on the road. You can't blind other drivers if you want safe travels for yourself. You achieve success by helping others succeed. The more you help others achieve success, the more success you will attract into your own life. If you go through life using pencil beams to guide you, you are likely to end up on dead-end streets with a group of friends who are pencil-beaming, too—if you have friends at all.

Fog Lights

Fog lights are typically offered as an extra feature on most vehicles or can be an aftermarket add-on. These lights are designed to be aimed low at the road to maximize visibility in varying types of weather. Sometimes, it's necessary to turn on the fog lights. This is when life throws things at you that you didn't see coming. This is when visibility is at its lowest, and when you feel you've lost sight of what you want and who you are.

Don't let this stop you from continuing on your journey. Consider this as a challenge to see what you are equipped with and an opportunity for growth. The wonderful thing about holding a vision is that you have the ability to see it in your mind, regardless of the external circumstances. Turn on the fog lights when you are at your darkest point, and I guarantee you will be able to see things you couldn't see before, and you will be guaranteed to make it through even the darkest of nights.

WIPERS

Windshield wipers are designed to remove rain and debris from your windshield. Imagine driving in the rain or snow without functioning wipers. Unfortunately, most people wait until they can barely see to replace old, worn-out wipers. Also, it's necessary to clean your windshield on the inside in addition to changing your wipers so you can have a clearer vision of what's ahead in stormy weather. If you are having trouble seeing and the windshield wipers are working properly, the problem could be on the inside.

All the perceived problems we encounter are made better or worse by our own minds. If you really want to master all the elements, invest in some good wipers. You attract to you what you choose to focus on regularly. So if you don't learn to wipe away negative thoughts, you're in for a dangerous ride! If you don't learn to wipe away mud splattered on your windshield, your visibility will be drastically impaired.

How often do you focus on the one bug that splattered on your windshield as opposed to the sun, trees, mountains, and other scenery around you in your travels? While it can be annoying, we often put our focus on this one mishap. We tend to overlook the beauty all around us and focus on the negative things that happen on our journey.

If you are guilty of this, start using your wipers and enjoy the beauty around you instead of focusing on the splattered bug. We often curse the poor bug that met its demise against our windshield, but have you ever stopped to think about the poor bug? Its journey is over. The people who try to "bug" you with negativity and criticism are not in a good place themselves. They are using their pencil beams to try to blind you from your own capabilities and run you off the road of success.

Creating negativity for others sabotages *you* because you get back what you put out. It puts you on a frequency to receive negativity and not the good things you desire. When you go to bed at night and find yourself focusing on the negatives, envision your wipers clearing it away and let it all go. This is called maintenance of your vision.

COOLANT

Coolant is a fluid which flows through or around a device to prevent it from overheating. A good coolant is said to have high thermal capacity, low velocity, is nontoxic, and neither causes nor promotes corrosion of the cooling system. Given this description, it's evident that a good coolant is vital to your car's performance. Therefore, a regular maintenance check on the coolant is a must.

How well do you keep your cool? Is there someone or something in your life who seems to know exactly what to say or do that pushes your buttons and gets you heated?

While anger is a natural, human emotion, too much of it for long periods of time indicates you are handing over your keys of emotional well-being and peace to someone or something else. This is especially true if this happens repetitively with the same person or situation. When this happens, you are basically allowing someone else to drive you "mad." No one can steer you to Anger Street if they are not behind the wheel of your car.

Allowing others to drive you "mad" changes your frequency, which will automatically attract more things to be mad about. Again, while anger is a natural, human emotion, falling victim to it repetitively subjects you to a long road of heartache and unhappiness. If you want to get angry, get angry enough to refuse to give others control over your emotions. Refuse to let anyone or anything steal your joy and peace of mind. Stop handing over the keys. Put your foot on the brake and declare enough is enough. You control your emotions, and you are in the driver's seat! Stop letting others drive you mad! Keep your cool, and don't even get into the same car with others who are attempting to sabotage you. Remind yourself that is not your car and not your journey, and steer clear of them. Keep focused on where you are going. Why in the world would you ever voluntarily jump into a car with someone going nowhere when you have your own car?

So, make sure you have plenty of coolant to keep your engine from overheating. By maintaining your cool, you accelerate much faster toward your goals and cruise through life without becoming wrecked by people or external circumstances. Let others' negativity and attempts to stall you fuel you.

OIL

Motor oil serves as a lubricant for your engine and allows components to pass through each other with limited amounts of friction. As you may be aware, friction between you and others can cause you to transfer focus from your goals onto the conflict, therefore letting your emotions get the best of you. It's essential that you regularly change the oil and filter in your car. If this is neglected, you can bet you will experience some major problems.

Basically, motor oil creates a small barrier between the parts in order for them to slide past one another. This increases efficiency, power, and performance. Are you able to let things slide by, or do you tend to swerve toward conflict, dwelling and spinning your wheels on what has happened? How well do you set boundaries with others? Have you heard the saying that you teach others how to treat you? What you allow from others will continue to show up in your experience.

If you tend to get all clogged up with others' nonsense, you may need to change your oil regularly. Stop falling victim to dipsticks. It's nearly impossible to be frustrated, angry, and resentful for long periods of time without it creating significant problems for you under your hood. Just as you could not travel 25,000 miles without an oil change in your car, you cannot continue to drive on negativity and ill feelings and not be a detriment to yourself.

It's essential that we maintain clean oil in our car. By clean oil, I mean clean boundaries with others and the ability to manage conflict without allowing it to drain or pollute you. Don't stall out when it comes to standing up for yourself or pushing the brake on nonsense. Filter your focus. Filter who you spend your time with. Perhaps 2,500 miles is all you can travel with a certain person.

Another function of motor oil is that it cools the upper portion of your engine. It does so by circulating while dissipating the heat throughout the journey. This cooling also reduces friction. Anger serves as an indicator of the things we do not want or like. However, hanging on to anger for any significant amount of time can destroy you. Instead of being angry about the things that have happened that you did not want or ask for, consciously change your focus to what you *do* want and what you *do* like. This is as simple as changing the gearshift from reverse to drive.

What type of oil do you use? What do you think about or do that calms you and keeps you feeling peaceful? How long does it take you to get out of someone else's car when they are driving you somewhere you don't want to go?

You maintain your life with your mind, and you are either the driver or the passenger. Which one are you, and what are

Driving Yourself Successful

you going to do about it? Not changing the oil dilutes it, causing rapid engine wear and tear that can result in increased emissions, fuel economy, and rapid oil consumption. In other words, dwelling on conflict, not setting boundaries, not standing up for yourself, and allowing yourself to be a passenger in someone else's car can lead to the inability to realize your dreams, increased outbursts with others, loss of money in your pocket, and could even drive you to consuming things that aren't good for you.

FUEL FILTER

Your fuel filter is on continuous duty whenever your ignition is running. It prevents impurities from clogging the injections. Fuel filters become obstructed due to dirt or rust in the fuel tank. A sign of a clogged filter is if the vehicle stalls when climbing hills.

Changing your fuel filter can be tricky and requires continued, conscious effort. You have already read the chapter that helped you determine what type of fuel you are using; now you will learn how to maintain the fuel filter. You will discover the importance of filtering how you react to outside circumstances so that your engine runs smooth and you don't become tainted or slowed down by outside dirt. In other words, maintaining a clean filter ensures your *power*.

Do you feel you are losing momentum while climbing the ladder to success? Does it sometimes seem that the harder you try the harder it gets, and everything seems like an uphill battle and you don't have the power to climb it?

If you have experienced a decrease in performance and ability to move forward, it may be time to replace your fuel filter because it could be clogged with faulty thinking and dirt from the outside world. The following steps will guide you in changing your fuel filter.

Step 1 is to purchase a new filter. This happens when you realize you have a clogged filter.

Step 2 is to locate the old filter. What's wrong with it? How do you know it's clogged? Are you stalling? Sputtering? Constantly upset? These are all good indicators of a clogged filter.

Step 3 is to remove the fuel pressure, if needed. Are you at the point of blowing a gasket? Before replacing the filter, you must get yourself into a better mind-set by talking to others, exercising, meditating, listening to music, etc. Give yourself permission to take whatever amount of time it takes to release the pressure.

Step 4 is to unscrew each hose clamp bolt until it comes apart from the nuts. In other words, begin to break free from things or people that upset you. You probably will have an internal reaction reading this section, which will serve as an indicator of who you need to detach from.

Step 5 is to push the clamp up the hose. Clamp down on making these important changes in your life.

Step 6 is to remove the old filter and replace with the new filter. This sounds simple, but it is where the pertinent work is done. This is where you must be patient with yourself.

Now, you have an increased awareness as to what is creating your discord and clogging your filter. Pay attention to how you're feeling. Be aware when your dash lights up, letting you know something is having a negative impact on your thinking. At the moment you recognize you are feeling anxious, depressed, angry, or any other negative emotion, retrace your thoughts. This is where you will find the culprit for your negative emotions. Filter your thinking so that minimal amounts of negativity ever enter into your thought stream. A good, clean filter makes for a smooth running car.

Step 7 is to push the clamps back down and tighten them. Once you discover how to consciously filter your thoughts, push down the clamps and tighten your grip! You definitely want them to stay in place. If you realized how much power your thoughts have in creating your reality, you would be afraid to ever think another negative thought again! By filtering your fuel, you equip yourself with enough gas to go wherever you want to go, and you'll get there much more smoothly than driving with a clogged filter.

Every day, you filter your thoughts and experiences. The parts that get through will stick with you and either increase or decrease your performance. I challenge you to examine what's passing through your filter. Shine your lights on these things and run them out of the road. Use your pencil beams to blind negativity from entering your operating system. A fresh, new filter creates a fresh, new perspective. Once you get a clear perspective, you are guaranteed to climb the hills with ease and full power.

TIMING BELT

The timing belt on your car keeps valves from bashing into pistons. When the belt fails, your forward progress will cease. Most of us say to ourselves that it's not the right time to do something, and we put it off. Napoleon Hill stated, "Begin at once—the time will never be just right." There may be a million reasons why you think something will not work, but all you really need is one reason it will. Do you need to adjust your timing belt? What excuses are you using that keep you from pursuing your dreams?

It's not necessary for you to know every single step. Just get started! Dream dreams large enough that you have no earthly idea how you will accomplish them. All you have to do is start where you are with what you have and take the first step in faith. Back out of the driveway and start driving. Now you are getting somewhere!

BATTERY

Even if you keep your terminals clean and your charging system works fine, you'll eventually have to change your battery. If you remember from Chapter 1, it's important to assess and remove the battery drainers from your life as well as to connect to a positive battery to recharge. Even if you started out with what you thought were battery chargers, things may have changed. Batteries do need to be replaced from time to time. Sometimes, we outgrow people. This tends to happen when you make a conscious effort to increase your own personal growth and development.

Some people feel guilty and stop growing, never realizing their true potential. Don't let anyone hold you back. It could be their own insecurities, jealousy, or fear of losing you that causes them to try to drain your battery. Going for your dreams despite adversity and negative interactions from others will inspire others that they, too, can do the same. A fresh start, just like a fresh battery, can be a life changer. It can completely revive your engine and get you moving closer to your desired destination. A tip to remember is to use a battery that matches the manufacturer's specifications. You are the manufacturer— what are your specs?

ALIGNMENT

Have you ever been driving down the road and hit an unexpected pothole that felt as if it had destroyed your car? Potholes have the potential to knock your car out of alignment. When this happens, it's necessary to take your car to a garage and have it realigned. What do you think will happen if you continue to hit potholes when your car is already out of alignment? Most likely, you won't be able to hold the wheel steady, and it'll cause you to veer off in the wrong direction. It could even cause you to wreck, potentially harming yourself or others as a result. You don't want your car to end up like this, and you should take appropriate actions to remedy the problem before it gets too damaging.

Think about the potholes you've hit in life. Sometimes they come out of nowhere and throw you off balance. They may cause you to go in a different direction, perhaps one that is not good for you. Maybe the potholes aren't unexpected ones but occurrences in your everyday life that have decreased your alignment with who you really are or what you really want.

What happens when you don't take action to regain your balance? If you are out of balance or "alignment," you are likely to feel uneasy, frustrated, out of sorts, and not yourself. It can cause you to lose motivation and energy. Failing to diagnose and treat the issue puts you at risk of major problems down the road.

Do you feel out of balance? Do you feel out of alignment with your authentic self or what you want in life? Perhaps you've hit too many potholes and are unsure of how to proceed. Once you recognize you are out of alignment, you need to start performing the maintenance necessary to get yourself back into optimal power.

You ask, "How do I get myself back into alignment?" It's really a simple concept but so difficult for a lot of people to actually practice. Most people will continue driving despite the difficulties they are experiencing, thinking that a little more effort will get them to their destination. While this is true in a lot of situations, it's not necessarily true in this case. You can't run on a broken leg and expect it to get stronger.

Some people just park the car and abandon all efforts to keep going. Obviously, this isn't going to work. So how do you do it? Imagine every thought you think carrying with it an energy frequency and that what you transmit, you receive an equivalent match in return. If you're feeling out of alignment, you're thinking thoughts that don't match the energy frequency of who you are and what you want. You must match the frequency of what you want and who you want to become with the thoughts you think. It's a simple concept, but difficult for many people because they become more focused on the potholes than the direction in which they are going. The moment you take your focus off what you want and who you want to become, you transmit frequencies of defeat, fear, doubt, and anxiety in which the universe will respond, sending you the equivalent matches for those feelings. In other words, you will encounter more potholes.

You have the power to change your thoughts at any given point in time. Right now, you can change your thought patterns—or frequency. You have the power to raise your energy level by simply choosing your next thought. This takes a conscious effort. This conscious effort and awareness is an indicator that you are now awake at the wheel. Try it. Start thinking the best-feeling thoughts you can imagine. Use your imagination to visualize a remarkable life filled with beauty, love, peace, and financial abundance or whatever else you desire. Happiness is just a thought away.

By engaging in regular maintenance, you ensure you will reach your full potential. By failing to do so, you set yourself up for significant problems down the road. Refuse to allow yourself to feel guilty about taking care of yourself. If someone else gets mad because you are spending time changing the oil in your car, you probably would laugh at them and keep going. If someone is offended by your level of self-care, it may be time to steer clear of them.

Replace what needs to be replaced and remove what no longer works. Align yourself with people who raise your energy level and don't deplete it. Life is too short to spend it with battery drainers who don't have your best interests in mind.

Regular maintenance ensures optimal performance, smooth driving, and increased personal power. The wonderful thing about maintenance is that there are only a few things that every vehicle needs, and almost all of them you can do yourself. Now that's horsepower!

CHECKPOINTS

1. Give yourself permission to create a healthy balance of work and play.

2. Shine light on your excuses and identify areas that need your attention. Make yourself a priority!

3. Align your thoughts and actions with your desires and who you aspire to be.

4. Check your fuel filter. Assess how well you are refusing to let impurities clog you emotionally. Filter your thinking so that minimal amounts of negativity enter into your thought stream.

5. A clear perspective ensures the climbing of hills with ease and full power.

6. Every thought transmits a frequency, and what returns in your experience is the equivalent match of this frequency. Consciously choose your thoughts. Begin by thinking the best-feeling thoughts that you can imagine; by doing so, you will experience the good feelings and experiences you desire.

Ignite Your Spark

Spark plugs in an automobile deliver the spark needed to ignite the air/fuel mixture and are considered the "business" end of the ignition system. No spark means no combustion, wasted energy, performance loss, idle roughness, hesitation, hard starting, and possibly even no start at all.

Let's define "spark" in this context as abundant energy, contagious enthusiasm, overwhelming excitement, confident eagerness, and fearless acceleration. Given this description, let me ask—are your sparks plugged? Do you feel you've lost your spark? Have you lost the motivation to set goals and the drive to accomplish them? Do you feel you've lost the energy and enthusiasm you once had? Have you lost the eagerness to take the necessary steps to begin? Have you lost confidence in yourself and your abilities? Perhaps you are one of many individuals who have allowed negative, distorted thinking to take the wheel of your life. Let's take a closer look at how sparks are created or destroyed.

Gasoline engines rely on spark plugs to ignite fuel. So, even with a full tank of gas, if there's no spark the car won't run! Are you running through life on negativity that has left you feeling empty inside? If so, this explains why you've never arrived at your desired destination! If you meet this criteria, there is hope to not only regain your spark, but to ignite your engine with more horsepower and drive than you've ever experienced!

All it takes is one single, fouled spark plug to kill up to 25 percent of a four-cylinder engine's power output. It works the same for our thoughts. All it takes is one single, negative thought to diminish our motivation, waste our energy, and impair our performance. One small, negative thought can accelerate into complete emotional disruption and idle roughness!

It's interesting to know that small spark plugs control the entire car's function! You may think that a small random thought has no lasting impact on your life. However, the beginning of greatness and failure begins with a single, isolated thought! That one negative thought tends to breed more negative, self-defeating thoughts, and before you know it you've begun a downward spiral and decelerated from your goals.

Our thoughts drive us to either accomplish great things or to wind up on a series of dead-end streets. These dead-end streets are completely self-made and do not exist in reality! Anyone can put up a street sign that reads "dead end," even though the path leads to great places. Where you end up will depend on your perceptions of yourself and others. Negative thoughts detour us from our dreams. If one negative spark plug can reduce power output by 25 percent, imagine what a series of negative thoughts can do to us! Driving through life fueled with negativity is like a car going downhill without brakes. It gets faster and faster, more out of control, and ends up wrecked!

What happens to our spark? Sometimes, it's hard to find because it becomes hidden in darkness. Other times, we simply get burnt out. Once burnout occurs, it's often difficult for us to reignite. However, "difficult" is not synonymous with "impossible." We may start out with a spark, but allow it to die out because of rejection or temporary defeat. So, we may possess the spark, but we don't accompany it with the necessary actions.

Unfortunately, many people allow others or circumstances to diminish their enthusiasm and zest for life. Perhaps they've driven through life with too many battery drainers. We often give in too easy. If others give up on us, we often give up on ourselves.

It's important to acknowledge and remember that the way others treat us does not define who we are and what we are capable of accomplishing. Accept that not everyone is going to share your vision. There will be those who tell you what you're doing isn't possible because they don't see *themselves* as having the capabilities to accomplish it. Spark plugs are relatively inexpensive and quite simple to replace; however, they can cost us everything if they stop working. So the question remains, how do you regain your spark?

TROUBLESHOOTING

Spark plugs can be described as the "window" into your engine and are a very valuable diagnostic tool to recognize potential problems you may not be able to otherwise identify. The spark plug may display symptoms and/or conditions of the engine's performance, and these symptoms can be analyzed to track down the root cause of many problems. If you feel you've "lost your spark," you must first utilize the shovel located in your trunk to uncover whatever caused it to become plugged. You must then dig deep under the hood to determine which spark plug has burned out. Perhaps the culprit is an item stored in your trunk that plugged your spark, such as a bad relationship, loss, or rejection.

By uncovering and acknowledging the area that caused your energy and enthusiasm to diminish, you are no longer lost in the dark. Once you shine light on the cause of the burnout, you acquire the power to reignite with newfound awareness and insight. By shining light on the path that got you nowhere, you can then renavigate your direction. Let's examine some potential causes for spark plugs to burn out.

1. Too Much Driving at Low Speeds or Idling for a Long Time

We can become so accustomed to a routine that we fail to improve mentally, physically, spiritually, socially, and professionally. We may feel we're doing our best but continue to experience disappointment. It's common to get to a place where you know what you want, but you have no idea how to get there. This is the point where you may say to yourself, "someday I will" or "one day."

As long as you continue using that language, "someday" will never arrive. To reinforce this, look for "someday" on your calendar. It doesn't exist! When you become stagnant and take the passive passenger approach to life, you allow life to pass you by and then, one day, ask yourself, "What happened to me?" This is a rut that can take years to get out of—if one ever chooses to do so! The key word in the previous sentence is "choose." You have a choice each and every day to make the best out of every situation and circumstance. You have a choice how you want to be and feel. You have a choice whether you drive through life without a set direction or whether you sit in the passenger seat. You have a choice whether or not you "idle" through your days. Wake up! The time is *now!* Stop idling and try to operate on burned-out spark plugs! Put your foot down to negativity and defeat and get going in a new direction!

It's absolutely necessary to develop a specific action plan to get started. Be sure to include a specific deadline as to when you will accomplish a task. Give yourself some checkpoints to make sure you are staying on route. Every morning, write down a specific goal you want to accomplish that day, and get it done! Idlers are those who either don't specify their goals or fail to make the necessary effort to accomplish them. Ask yourself each day if you are accelerating or idling. Staying on the road to your dreams and celebrating each and every small accomplishment will ensure your spark doesn't burn out!

2. Oil Leaking into the Cylinders

Oil leaks are *never* a good thing to have happen—especially when the oil causes damage to an area that controls the functioning of the entire car! Too much oil in the unit, leaky valves, faulty rubber grommets, bad piston rings, and a faulty head gasket are all potential causes for leaking oil.

Negativity can flow in from all directions and directly impact the cylinders we run on each day. To begin to fix the problem of leakage, get rid of the excess oil, or should I say *negativity!* Sometimes this means letting go of people, places, and things that contaminate you. Who are the people you perceive as causing you to lose your spark and ability to function at your highest potential? What are the circumstances or environmental factors that plug your spark? In case you didn't know, oil and water do not mix; however, both have their purposes.

Let's consider water as being healthy and oil, on the other hand, as not. However, both depend on the context to which they are being referred. Even water can be deadly under certain circumstances, and oil is a vital substance needed to keep the car running smoothly. Learn to say goodbye to negative, toxic people, but realize they also served a purpose in your life. Don't continue to focus on the pain they may have caused you. Instead, purposefully relocate them to a place that doesn't inhibit your current level of functioning but fuels your willpower to succeed. Program your mind to focus on the good you desire in your life, and allow those to be your dominate thoughts. You can't get clean water if you keep putting oil into the glass!

3. Poorly Adjusted or Worn Valves

The only thing certain in life is change. Unfortunately, many people have difficulty adjusting to life's detours. Some pull over beside the road and refuse to continue because they are unsure of what lies ahead. Some start out on a new road but return to the old one because they prefer to stick to what's comfortable. By choosing either of these roads, you allow potential defeat and cling to the mistaken belief that you couldn't go any farther.

Not doing something and not being able to are two different concepts. Many people are trapped in their wrecked cars with these beliefs, and sometimes even the "jaws of life" can't bring them out unless they cooperate by choosing to change their belief system. Changing your belief system is something you must do yourself! No one else can do this for you!

The biggest reason people struggle with change is their underlying, erroneous belief that they can't handle what they perceive is going to happen or may happen. So many people have traveled the same streets of Heartache, Pain, and Defeat that they have become worn. When people become worn, they lose their spark. When people lose their spark, they tend to search for anything to reignite it.

Often, people look in all the wrong places to reignite their spark. This then leads them down the streets of Disappointment and Unfulfillment. Depending on others or changes in your circumstances to regain your spark will leave you dim, worn, and resentful.

To regain your spark and ensure better adjustment to any situation life may bring, the most beneficial tool you possess is your own mind. The thoughts that drive through your mind will pave the road for either adjustment or maladjustment and will dictate whether you are drained of energy and effectiveness or fully equipped with abundant energy and fearless acceleration in the direction of your goals.

4. Engine Overheating

If steam spews from underneath your hood, your engine is overheating. If this occurs on a regular basis, it's time for a complete tune-up! Allowing your engine to overheat can cause disastrous damage to the internal engine components and cost you a fortune in repairs! Contrary to what you may think, spark plugs cannot create heat, they can only remove it! The spark plug serves as a heat exchanger, pulling unwanted thermal energy away from the combustion chamber and transferring the heat to the engine's cooling system. The *heat range* is a plug's ability to dissipate heat. When an engine becomes overheated, combustion of gasoline can occur in places other than the combustion chamber; when this happens, it's referred to as "detonation."

Detonation can lead to a complete meltdown of the ground strap of the spark plug. The higher the heat, the more damage is done and can potentially remain—even after the engine has cooled.

How often does your engine overheat? Do you let people push your buttons to the point you feel as if smoke is coming out of your ears? Do you feel like a victim of circumstance and others' actions to the point you have become angry and resentful? Whom do you allow to detonate your emotions? It's clear that an overheated engine can severely damage your spark. How can you have a healthy spark if you are void of energy, enthusiasm, excitement, eagerness, and fearless acceleration?

Refuse to allow others to detonate you! When we realize people only have control over us if we allow them to, we can begin to activate our own cooling system, which will prevent our engines from overheating. We can't control the words or actions of others or how they might direct them at us, but we *can* control how we respond, which enables us to remain powerful in the driver's seat of our emotions.

Imagine this scenario. A person in another state is talking all sorts of nonsense about you at this very moment. However, you are not aware of this, so your mood remains unaffected.

The fact that this person is saying terrible things about you doesn't have the power to directly influence your mood. Thus, we can safely say that A≠C. On the other hand, let's say this person is in the next room, and you can hear all the negative things being said. How would this affect your mood? Would you become angry and upset? Would your self-esteem take a hit? Would you "fly off the handle" when you see them? If you answered "yes" to any of these questions, you are not alone. However, true mastery of self involves the ability to not jump in the car with someone else on their journey. If someone is upset with you and saying negative things about you, it's about them, not you! Make a conscious decision to *let it go!* Instead of allowing it to dull your spark, let it fuel you!

All too often, we tend to let others dictate our emotional journey and sense of self-worth. Words are words until you give them meaning—which can also translate to *power*.

Remember, you have no control over others, but you *do* have control over yourself and how you respond. Do not allow others to detonate negative emotions in you. This damages *your* spark, not theirs. From this point forward, *stop* at the intersection of Overheating and Revenge, and take a right turn onto Peace Street.

5. Gap Is Too Wide

No doubt about it, life can throw us some curveballs. Unexpected events and circumstances can present themselves to us and force us to take detours from our original plan. It's not uncommon for people to stay stagnant after a detour and spend many years idling.

Perhaps you are the mom who became pregnant at a young age and didn't finish your education. Maybe you're the son who had to quit college to pursue full-time employment to care for your family. Perhaps you got lost and went in a bad direction for quite some distance. Maybe it's been years since you've been in a committed relationship, and you think it's too late for you because of your age or a previous divorce or any other reason.

Something else that can cause our spark to burn out is too wide of a gap between life events. We can make ourselves believe all sorts of irrational things about ourselves, and it usually doesn't take much to convince us of the obstacles and perceived defeat that appear to lie ahead. You may say to yourself that it's "too late" or "too much time has passed." It's time to regain your spark by refusing to tell yourself you're too old to get your education. It's time to stop telling yourself you have too much going on to pursue the desires of your heart. It's time to stop telling yourself you have been single too long and, therefore, have lost your appeal.

It doesn't matter how much time has already passed! It's never too late to begin again! Set new goals or work toward those that have taken a backseat!

A sufficient amount of voltage must be supplied by the ignition system to cause the spark to jump across the spark plug gap, thus creating what is called "electrical performance." When you give yourself a boost, you ignite your spark! Get going—your happiness is waiting!

6. Incorrect Timing

Most of us have probably had the experience of saying or doing something at the wrong time. When this happens, it can lead to feelings of embarrassment and all sorts of negative self-talk that inhibits us from moving forward with self-confidence.

Doing something at the wrong time and not achieving the desired results can cause us to lose our spark and diminish our belief in our ability to succeed. Then, we often give up and refuse to travel down that same road again.

It's important to remember that to everything there is a season and that things work out in the right time. Some people establish the belief that something is not meant to happen after they have tried something at the wrong time. Things work when they are *supposed* to work and not a moment sooner. The fact that you tried something in the past and it didn't work then does not necessarily mean it won't work now.

Let's look at a relationship, for example. Maybe you invested yourself in a relationship that ended very badly. Maybe you've even had several relationships that have all ended badly. Perhaps it wasn't the right time in your life for a serious relationship because you had to learn who you were and build the necessary strength and independence you needed to be able to stand alone first.

It may be that you haven't been able to find your way off Heartache Street, and you are frantically looking in the rearview mirror at Relationship Road and swearing you'll never travel there again. The fact that a relationship didn't work out in the past doesn't mean you are incapable of experiencing happiness in a new relationship. It could be that *now* is a better time and place for a new relationship because of the growth you've experienced.

Stop living in the past and sitting beside the road in your parked car! You hold the keys to your future, and only you can create the scenery.

One can relate this scenario to a car in the wrong place at the wrong time that became involved in a minor accident the driver didn't even see coming. This doesn't mean the driver never gets behind the wheel again. It means that after some repair work the driver is able to get back on the road of life with improved vigilance. The driver now has more experience as to what to watch out for and how to avoid a potentially hazardous situation.

There are many famous people who have created great things that have positively impacted the lives of others. Those who never gave up despite facing many collisions along their road to success. The time may never feel right, but start where you are with what you have, and go for it! Incorrect timing doesn't mean "never." There are countless roads of possibilities in life, and all you have to do is be willing to take the journey!

7. Replace the Plugs

Now that we've examined some possible causes for sparks to burn out, let's look at some added tools to ensure your spark gets reignited. In order to reignite your spark, you must pull the plug on self-destructive thought patterns. Every single thing in life starts with a thought, and thoughts repeated become beliefs. We will get what we *believe*—whether accurate or not! To regain your spark, you must find it within yourself to *believe* it's possible to regain your spark. Until you believe something is possible, it will never come to pass!

If you don't believe you are capable of having the car you always wanted, you'll never have it. If you don't *believe* you'll ever be "lucky enough" to have a nice home with money in the bank, you'll never have it. If you don't *believe* you can be with someone you can trust and find happiness with, you'll never find that person. If you don't *believe* you can drive, you'll never get behind the wheel.

You've probably heard the saying, "If it ain't broke, don't fix it." However, there are times when you may not realize something is broken, or maybe it doesn't appear broken, but it nonetheless *needs* fixing. However, once you become aware something is actually broken, it's time to fix it!

Using a spark plug socket, remove each burned-out plug from the engine and replace it with a new spark plug. A very important step in replacing spark plugs is to clean all debris from around the plug. Start cleaning out the debris from your life. Clean out your trunk. Clear your mind of clutter, doubt, fear, defeat, and inferiority.

Debris may be in the form of people, places, things, or your environment. "Sock it" to negative thoughts, and make space for the "you" that is waiting to arrive! Just because the sun may be hidden behind the clouds doesn't mean it fails to exist! You may not be able to see underneath the hood of your car, but there is an engine that can take you from Point A to Point B and anywhere in between if you give it the right kind of fuel!

LIVE YOUR PASSION

What brings you the most enjoyment in life? What makes you smile? What revs your engine and makes you want to put the pedal to the metal? What dream have you held in your heart since childhood that you or someone else talked you out of pursuing? Could it be you had a vision for yourself but later believed that vision was too far-fetched to ever come true, and thus, you parked that vision in the junkyard? Maybe you're afraid to envision the life you really want because your under-lying belief is that it will never happen and you want to spare yourself the disappointment.

If this is your make and model, you must realize that you have nothing to lose! If you don't have what you really want in life, remember that you'll remain in the same place if you don't start the car! However, you *will* get a short distance down the road if you at least crank the car and begin driving—even if you don't know exactly where you're going or how to get there.

When you shine light on whatever makes you feel alive, you'll ignite the spark within you that puts you on the road to countless opportunities, abundance, and fulfillment. Pull the plug on impossible! If you have a passion for something, the desire to make it happen, and the determination and willpower to stay the course despite detours, there is absolutely nothing you cannot achieve! Detours are for your protection or to help steer you in a different direction—not to make you pull over and park! Stay in the driver's seat and keep moving forward, even if you go in a different direction than initially planned!

When driving through life, the key is to be flexible. Some-times wrong turns take us on rides we'll never forget and bring great beauty and meaning to our journey that would never have been on the route we mapped out for ourselves. You will begin to realize that there were never really any wrong turns, only necessary roads to travel in order to enrich your journey.

When you install within your own mind-set an antilock breaking system, you'll never fail to arrive at your destination. Develop a clear vision of what you want, fuel yourself with pos-itive affirmations and faith to achieve it, and accelerate in the direction you've mapped out for yourself. In other words, get in the car, gas up with premium fuel, start driving, and don't stop until you get there! Don't be deterred by wrong turns or detours, and most importantly, keep driving!

It's essential to refuel before you run out of gas. At this point, if you have a spark but no fuel, you're stuck. Remember, gasoline engines rely on spark plugs to ignite the fuel. As long as you continue to use the appropriate fuel and maintain your spark, you will arrive at your desired destination.

CHECKPOINTS

1. Determine what or who you perceive caused you to lose your spark. Recognize you have all the power within to reignite it despite your past experiences.

2. Ask yourself each day if you are idling or accelerating.

3. Learn to say goodbye to negative, toxic people. Choose to focus on your personal power to succeed and use your experiences as fuel to move forward.

4. To reignite your spark and ensure adjustment to any situation life may throw at you, the most beneficial tool you possess is your own mind. Pull the plug on self-destructive thought patterns.

5. Refuse to let others detonate you as this takes away your power.

6. It's never too late to begin again. Set new goals and work toward the ones that have taken a backseat.

DEVELOP AND MAINTAIN CLEAR VISION

Have you ever been driving on a wet road and the mud slung from another person's car splattered your windshield, making it difficult to see where you're going? You were probably feeling frustrated and anxious—maybe even scared—due to decreased visibility.

This is often how we feel when we don't have a clear picture, or vision, of what we want in life. It's sometimes hard for us to picture how we want our future to look and, even more puzzling, how to get there.

How can you get where you're going if your vision is hindered? How do you know when you've arrived at your destination if you don't know where you're going? Has someone blocked your vision for your future with a negative or selfish comment? Perhaps you've been told the following: "You can't do that!" "I think you should do this." "Don't get above your raising." "Why on earth would you want to do that?"

If you've been told any of these things, you know firsthand how hurtful it can be. These types of unwarranted comments often put the brakes on the visions we have for ourselves. Our goals become minimized and washed away like wiper blades wiping away rain. Without a goal or destination, we are merely ships with no sail, birds without wings, and cars with no gas.

Perhaps it's not mud splattered from someone else's car that interferes with your visibility. It could be that you are driving through hail. Don't let a little hail damage your vision for your future. Don't let a little hail crack your self-esteem.

If the "hail" you've been through has already damaged your self-esteem and visibility, pull over and reevaluate the situation. When you stop and examine the situation closely and look at things from the inside out, you can begin to reprogram your life's direction and start moving toward it with much more clarity and drive. You can do this despite the hail still coming at you from all directions.

To reiterate from a previous chapter, we can't always control the events or circumstances that occur in our lives, but we do have 100 percent control over our thoughts and corresponding reactions to them! Therefore, there will never be a situation that you can't gain control over by choosing your thoughts and reactions wisely.

Emotional reactions are normal, but refuse to allow your emotions to keep you paralyzed with anger, resentment, or false representations of yourself. Use it as fuel to reassess and devise a greater plan. Don't continue to drive through life on cruise control, failing to adjust and reevaluate your progress and clear away whatever hinders your vision.

All too often, we let a small crack in the windshield deter us from pursuing our goals. A cracked windshield does not mean the car won't run. It simply means some time and effort must be taken in order to repair the damage and get the car back on the road.

Many people drive through life only looking in the rearview mirror. The past has such a strong hold on them that they're paralyzed from moving forward. They're stranded because of the bumpy road they just traveled and are too afraid to continue on their journey.

Imagine getting in your car, turning the key, putting the gearshift in drive, pushing the gas, and only looking in the rearview mirror. Do you think you're likely to arrive at your desired destination only looking at what's behind you? Do you think it's possible to drive through life not causing harm to yourself or others along the way? If you are only looking in the rearview mirror while driving, you are going to run into things that continue to inhibit your ability to get anywhere. You are likely to wreck your car and cause damage to yourself and others that will cost you dearly. When we drive, we must rely on our rearview mirror periodically to see what is coming up on us from behind and to see when we may need to change lanes. The key word is *periodically*. What is behind us can serve as our guide to where we decide to travel and when we need to change lanes. It does not dictate our destination.

While some may drive through life looking in the rearview mirror, others drive through life with their eyes closed, unable to see positivity and possibility. Imagine trying to drive your car with your eyes closed. Not only will you not get very far, but you're highly likely to crash in a very short time and get nowhere fast.

How many of us, figuratively speaking, drive through life with our eyes closed? Why are our eyes closed to positivity and opportunity but wide open to negativity and defeat? The answer is that we have programmed ourselves to get what we look for in life—good or bad.

If you just had a "headlight moment" where you realized this is you, you've just gained insight and awareness that will get you on the road to success! You can't change anything of which you are not aware.

Pull over, and begin to think of what characteristics and traits you look for in yourself and others. When you begin to shine headlights on this particular part of you, you'll start to see a clearer picture of why you see what you see and what has been leading to either happiness or disappointment for you.

Now, start looking for good. Begin to look for the good in yourself and others around you, even the other drivers who splatter mud on your windshield. Perhaps the mud was there as an opportunity for you to pull over and rethink your life and the direction it's going. When you become the observer and not just the participant, you'll see that a little mud, or even a little hail, is only temporary.

Take a moment and think of anyone who you perceive as having been detrimental to you in some way. Now, think about what they taught you. Did they make you more resilient? Did they teach you how *not* to be? Did they make you a stronger person? Look for the silver lining.

Napoleon Hill said, "Every adversity and defeat carries with it the seed of equal or greater benefit." If you think about it, you'll realize that along with the hurt and pain you've suffered, you've also developed a strong character and will to survive. The simple fact that you are reading this book proves it.

There've been many people who've turned negative life experiences into fuel to help others. Many who've experienced traumatic abuse histories, overwhelming loss, and rejection have been able to scoot into the driver's seat and pull others off dead-end streets and onto the road of possibilities and hope.

This is what it means to create supreme fuel from life's roadblocks and take the wheel toward your desired destination. You have a choice. You can either allow these experiences to destroy and junk your car, or you can syphon the pain and pump it as the positive fuel necessary for internal and external success. Look for ways in which you can use your experiences to benefit yourself and others. The truth is, what we do to others we, in turn, do to ourselves.

In times when we feel abandoned and alone, spending time with others and assisting them on *their* journey fills our tank so we can continue on our own journey. It can help us realize that we're not driving alone on a back road in the dark. Encourage someone who is struggling to see the light, for this brings you a brighter perspective as well.

If you've had trouble gaining a clear vision of how you want your future to be, *now* is the perfect time to start! Use this as an opportunity to imagine *whatever* you'd like, even if, at this point in time, you see no way in which to make it happen.

Go ahead! What do you imagine for yourself? Where do you desire to be? How do you desire to feel? What do you desire to become? There are no limits to what you can imagine! Nothing is impossible for the imagination!

Once you're able to envision what it is you truly want in life, fuel yourself with the appropriate positive affirmations and fearless actions to make it a reality. It will only become reality if you can clearly *see* it become reality. Clean your windshield, and prepare yourself for your journey toward success—whatever that looks like for you. Focus your awareness on this vision every single day. Post pictures of what you envision around your home. Maybe it's a new career, a new home, a specific amount of money, a fulfilling relationship, or anything else you want. Continue to focus on these pictures and see yourself already in possession of them. If you focus your attention on doubt or lack, you're setting yourself up for not accomplishing your dreams.

Don't become your own roadblock! Many times, it's ourselves—not others—who block our own road to success. Your car can't go where you don't steer it! You can't get to the next town by simply wishing you were there. You must first have faith in yourself and believe you can get there. Then, you must take appropriate action to arrive. Start by getting in your car. Turn the key, put it in drive, and give it some gas while steering in the right direction. No matter how long it takes, don't stop until you get there! You can't get anywhere driving on negative, self-defeating thoughts! These cause the car to stall and yield poor performance.

All too often, we take on the visions of what others project for us. This may be your parents telling you what you need to be when you grow up. Or maybe it's a partner or friend who lacks belief in themselves to achieve the goals you verbalized, so they project their self-doubt onto you.

Think about how many times you may have reduced the size of your dreams because of someone else's poor self-esteem and self-doubt! How often have you allowed others' insecurities to dictate who you are and what you are (or aren't) capable of achieving? Maybe this person is you!

Sometimes we decelerate our visions because we don't receive the positive feedback we desire. This reduces visibility just like fog lingering on a cool, fall morning. However, just because there's fog, this doesn't remove the beautiful scenery that may be momentarily hidden from view. You simply may have to wait for the fog to clear in order to get where you want to go. Are you living in a fog? Is there someone or something that has reduced your visibility? Turn on your fog lights and shine through it! You are the one who controls the switch.

Ralph Waldo Emerson said, "What lies behind us and what lies before us are tiny matters compared to what lies within us." No matter how the road appears ahead and no matter what roads you have already traveled, remember that you have greatness within! You are not defined by personal hardships or troubles, and your value as a person is not defined by any-one else's words or mistakes—unless you *allow* yourself to be defined this way. You hold the key to freedom! If your vision isn't clear, it's time to clean your windshield! The bug-splattered and muddy windshields are not accurate representations of what the windshield is truly capable of, just as your past experiences and mistakes are not accurate representations of who you really are. However, you will continue to see yourself, and life, with hindered visibility until you wipe it clean. You can't *drive yourself successful* with impaired vision! Only *you* have the power to maintain clear visibility! Once the windshield has been thoroughly cleaned, you'll begin to see yourself and the world around you clearly and accurately. You can now enjoy the lovely scenic views while acknowledging the beauty within you with 20/20 vision.

If you've been through bumps in the road, roadblocks, detours, and dead ends, now is the time to write your life experiences into a story of resilience. Re-authoring your life story this way not only helps you heal, but helps you prosper and reveals strengths you didn't even realize you had! It helps you clearly see what you're made of instead of the negative events that you've allowed to define you.

Consider this—isn't it rather remarkable that you have experienced the things you have been through and are still here today? There's never been a situation you didn't survive, right? You have conquered the winding roads and made it to your current destination. *You've made it this far*—through adversities and roadblocks of all kinds! The greatness within you can now be realized! The windshield is now clear! From this point forward, when you tell your life story, tell it from a new perspective. Tell your story from the viewpoint of perseverance and triumph. You've achieved victory over defeat! You've driven through hail and survived! You are an overcomer!

Driving through life will now be simpler and more fuel efficient with your now increased self-visibility! You're now equipped to go anywhere you want to go in life. Your gearshift no longer has to remain in park or you no longer have to sit in idle because you can't see where you're going. You're now on your way!

Focus on your resilience and how you've had the strength to move forward despite all life's hurtful situations. Steer your attention to persevering over the "hail" you've been through while reprogramming your GPS to new locations. If you must, take a different route and notice the beauty around you and *within* you. Focus on the power of the V8 engine instead of that one scratch on the windshield.

Once you realize you have the power to see things differently and more positively and you begin to reprogram your GPS, the dents and scratches will get smaller and smaller and your faith in yourself will grow larger and larger. You will begin to see yourself as the amazing, capable, unique individual you really are!

We are all in a constant state of creation. We are all reprogramming our GPS to get us to the next location. If you are not where you want to be, program in a new destination. *No matter where you are, you are never lost!* All roads lead to somewhere, but it's up to you to decide whether or not you turn around, keep driving, or pull over. There's *always* a route to get you where you want to go. Where you are now does not have to be where you end up. The choice is yours! Only you can decide the roads you'll travel. You're more likely to reach your destination with clear visibility and accurate directions!

One of the most powerful tools you can use to help you establish a clear direction in life is *visualization.* Visualization involves picturing yourself doing the things you want to do, feeling the way you want to feel, and being the person you want to be.

For example, let's say you want to be more self-confident. Close your eyes and envision yourself walking into a room filled with many people, and feel yourself being self-confident and self-assured. Really feel it. Allow yourself to feel all the positive emotions you have toward yourself with this new level of self-confidence. Imagine everything you'll accomplish as a result of this new you—the "you" that exists beneath the fog. Practice this regularly! The more you practice visualization, the faster those visualizations will become your reality!

Also, supplement your visualizations by acting "as if." The next meeting you attend, act *as if* you are already self-confident. The next time you have to confront a situation, act *as if* you have every right to state your observations and opinions—because you do!

Visualization can be applied to any area of your life—such as acquiring a career you desire, acing a job interview, speaking in public, etc. Picture over and over in your mind every detail *exactly* as you desire it to be. Envision *exactly* what you'll say and do. Envision living the life you desire. Envision yourself as successful. Envision yourself in the career you desire. Envision living in the home you desire. Envision the car you desire. Envision the relationships you desire. Envision the peace you desire. When you have a clear vision for your future, you create your own reality. You know where you are going and where you will arrive. You'll not stop midway and decide this is as far as you can go.

The reason most people do not achieve their dreams is because they cannot *imagine* themselves actually achieving them. Visualization accelerates you in the right direction and paves the road to success. Refuse to have a V8 engine and only travel through life at 25 miles per hour! Get out there and show yourself what you're truly made of—strength, perseverance, determination, persistence, and resiliency! It's your car and your journey! Don't hand over the keys to anyone who hinders your visibility. If you can envision it and believe it, you will most definitely achieve it!

CHECKPOINTS

1. If you are only looking in the rearview mirror while driving, you are going to run into things that continue to inhibit your ability to drive yourself to success.

2. Your past negative experiences can be used to improve your life as well as assist others on their journey. This is personal empowerment!

3. Use your imagination to your advantage, not your demise. Every day, visualize your life exactly the way you would like it to be.

4. Tell your story from a new perspective. You are a survivor! You have the power to see things differently at any point in time.

5. You create your own reality with your vision, beliefs, and actions!

STOP BLOWING SMOKE

Picture yourself getting into your car, cranking it up, and seeing a cloud of smoke in your rearview mirror. You may say to yourself, "Uh-oh! This is *not* good!" Perhaps you've driven many miles and haven't noticed the smoke coming from your exhaust, but another driver makes you aware of it. Whatever the case, smoke coming from your car is a sign of trouble and could potentially pose significant problems that could keep you from arriving at your destination.

What have you been saying you want to achieve? What have you been telling yourself, and others, you want to have or experience in life? Have you taken persistent action toward achieving your goals, or are you just simply talking about them—or blowing smoke?

It's time to examine your thoughts and behaviors to discover if your gearshift is in drive or neutral. If you perceive yourself as being in "drive," are you pushing the gas to get moving, or are you just sitting there idling? Perhaps you're talking a lot about where you want to go but haven't even set foot in your car.

So, stop blowing smoke and take action! It's time to get your drive back! It's time to stop being "exhausted" wanting your car to take you somewhere and, because of your own lack of drive, fretting because you're not there yet. It's much less tiring to drive toward what you want than to vent your unhappiness about the current state of your life. Complaining only attracts more things to complain about and leaves you stranded on the road to your dreams. Where you turn the steering wheel is where you'll end up! Make sure you're not turning down Complaint Avenue.

If you've just diagnosed yourself as a smoke blower, you have achieved the first step toward making necessary changes—awareness! You can't change what you are unaware of. Awareness is power. Now, you can create a definite plan to improve your performance and eliminate the smoke. Transform yourself from blowing smoke to smoking your greatest competitor—your negative thoughts!

To ensure your ability to drive yourself successful, let's bring awareness to what could be causing you to blow smoke.

BLOWN HEAD GASKET

The head gasket is an airtight seal between the engine block and the cylinder head. It provides a means of maintaining pressure in the engine, increasing the efficiency of the internal combustion system. Problems with your head gasket can cause your car to smoke. A blown head gasket can reduce the power produced by the cylinder, resulting in rough running and degraded performance. The head gasket allows for more fuel to be burned, thus releasing more power. If the energy is bad, it can be released through the broken seal, causing further power loss.

Every thought you think emits its own energy! The types of thoughts you have will drive your energy level. Defeating thoughts reduce energy while positive thoughts increase energy and momentum. If you're blowing smoke and venting about all the things that haven't gone right for you, or you're holding on to resentment, you're heading toward a blown head gasket! You are not using your head to serve you to your greatest potential! You are blowing your ability to move forward by focusing on the negatives. You must get your head in the right spot so you don't go through life blowing smoke—not getting where you want to go and exhausting yourself, and others, in the process!

CRACKED OR WARPED CYLINDER HEAD

One of the main causes of white exhaust smoke and coolant loss is a cracked or warped cylinder head. A cracked head may allow coolant to leak into the cylinders or into the combustion chambers of the engine. A poorly maintained cooling system, low coolant, or nonfunctioning cooling fan can cause engine overheating.

Do you ever lose your cool? Do you ever feel so angry and upset that smoke could shoot out your ears at any point? Perhaps you have a tendency to get upset because you're not where you want to be and, filled to the brim with jealousy, you watch others acquire or achieve the very things you desire.

Perhaps you've gotten yourself into a warped way of thinking—saying to yourself that you are not good enough, worthy enough, or talented enough to achieve your goals. Could you be sabotaging yourself by telling others about your dreams and desires but then, deep within yourself, not believing you can achieve them?

It's crucial that you become aware of and identify the warped things you are telling yourself about your potential—or lack of it. Self-sabotage can detour you straight to Anger and Resentment Street.

Dwelling on perceived failures and imagining potential failures increases feelings of anger and defeat. It also changes the vibrational frequency you transmit to the universe, which attracts to you more defeat and failure. Smoke coming from your exhaust isn't caused by an external force but is created internally—by your own thoughts! If you want the smoke to clear, clear your head cylinders. Identify cracks in your thinking, and seal them with hope and assurance for your future as well as genuine happiness for others' success. Realize that the universe is yielding to you for your greater good, but you must start cruising through life with enjoyment instead of road rage. You must feel good to receive the good!

FEAR

Fear may be the culprit causing you to blow smoke. Nothing can cause someone to give up on pursuing their dreams as potently as fear. You may be telling others your future plans, but underneath the hood you may be terrified to take action toward those plans you've talked about.

You may question yourself with, "What if I fail?" or "What if I can't handle it?"

You may even fear success as much as or more than failure! What happens if you actually achieve your dreams and you fear you can't sustain your success? If you've found yourself asking these questions, it's time to make a "fear shift." Stop paralyzing yourself with negative *what ifs*, and start accelerating with the *whens!* Get yourself in gear and move forward! Stop idling and just passing gas! You have what it takes so stop fueling yourself with doubt. Stop blowing smoke and leave defeating thoughts in the dust!

Now that we have that settled, let's look at the types of smoke you may be emitting and what each type means in terms of your success.

BLACK SMOKE

Black smoke is caused by excess fuel that has entered the cylinder area and cannot be burned completely. Burning of excess fuel is referred to as "running rich." Now, if one is experiencing a car that is blowing smoke, this seems like the best smoke to blow. Why? Because you can't ever fuel yourself with too much positivity!

If positivity is overflowing into your cylinders then you are more likely to be "running rich." You receive what you give out, and if money is your goal and you have gotten yourself to a place of feeling good, you *will* receive it. You *must* match the frequency of the reality you want in order to receive your desires. Go ahead! Excessively fuel yourself with good-feeling thoughts and experiences, for then you are truly running rich!

BLUE SMOKE

Blue smoke is caused by engine oil entering the cylinder area and being burned along with the fuel/air mixture. All it takes is a small drop of oil leaking into the cylinder to produce blue smoke from the tailpipe. Are you feeling blue? Have you allowed life's circumstances, events, or other people to leak into your mind and burn you? Has your thinking been altered so significantly that your mental health and well-being are compromised? It's imperative to guard yourself from these leaks! It's easy to let things get to you, but you must make a conscious effort to clean it up before it spills over and causes you to become blue and blow smoke!

WHITE SMOKE

White smoke is basically steam caused by water and antifreeze entering the cylinder and the engine trying to burn it with the fuel. Obviously, not everything is meant to go together. If there are people or things in your life that are counterproductive to your success and peace of mind, it's necessary to remove them if you want to live an optimal life.

Listen to your internal monitoring system—otherwise known as your gut. You know what's not right for you. In order to accelerate out of first gear you may have to make some difficult decisions for your greater good. On your journey, you may have to stop and let some people out. Sometimes you drive ahead while others stay parked. You owe it to yourself to remove anything or anyone that interferes with your happiness and well-being. Otherwise, your energy frequency decreases, and roadblocks to success are created. It's up to you to muster enough courage to let go of things that no longer serve you. It may not be easy, but it will definitely be worth it!

Life is stressful at times. Are you giving yourself opportunities to release some steam? Are you engaging in regular maintenance of your emotions so your engine doesn't try to burn bad fuel? Be assertive in expressing your wants and needs to others. Let go of the "fear shift" when it comes to standing up for yourself.

Lack of assertiveness can lead to resentment and exhaustion. It may cause you to run out of gas and become stranded somewhere you don't want to be. Assertiveness and courage lead to fulfillment of your desires and actualization of your authentic self.

Regardless of what type of smoke you may be blowing, you must recognize that a big cloud of smoke following you everywhere you go will not likely attract the things you want in life. This can lead others to avoid you, atmosphere pollution that makes you vulnerable to "in hell" the toxins, and eventually your car will stall completely, leaving you stranded on the road that could have taken you straight to success.

If you're going to talk about your dreams, then hold yourself accountable to take action, no matter how small the steps may seem. Keep moving! Creep if you have to, but keep moving forward. Don't be afraid to let go of fear or, if you must, move forward in spite of it.

Fear is only an imagined force preventing you from arriving at your destination. Use your imagination to your advantage, and envision what you want and how you'll feel once you receive or achieve it. Get your head in the right place. If you are looking backward and focused more on what you don't want, the past will keep repeating itself. Focus forward, to the grandest life you can imagine. Fuel yourself with so much positivity and possibility that it overflows, leaving defeating thoughts in a huge cloud of smoke.

See yourself as running rich and the universe will have no choice but to deliver you riches. Refuse to let others bring you down, but recognize that you will, most likely, meet with their attempts many times on your journey. Let them fuel you in the right direction instead of setting roadblocks for you. Don't be afraid to let go of things that no longer serve you. Letting go can be a powerful boost in the direction of your destiny! When you achieve your heart's desires, you will become grateful for everything, as it has helped accelerate you toward greatness!

Believe in yourself with everything you are equipped with—even if you're the only car on the road! Not everyone is going to dream your dream. That's okay. They're not supposed to! You don't need to be among a carload of passengers to get where you desire.

Your time is now! Stop blowing smoke over past situations that you allowed to make you angry, bitter, and doubtful! Leave all of it behind in the dust! Nelson Mandela stated, "As I walked out the door toward the gate that would lead to my freedom, I knew if I didn't leave my bitterness and hatred behind, I'd still be in prison." Refuse to stay a passive passenger in your own car. When the dust settles and the smoke clears, you'll be able to see clearly your new abundant life!

CHECKPOINTS

1. Smoke is created internally by your thoughts. Bring awareness to your thoughts and beliefs that are causing you to "blow smoke."

2. You must feel good to receive good.

3. Listen to your internal monitoring system—your gut.

4. Assertiveness and courage lead to fulfillment of your desires and actualization of your authentic self.

5. Fuel yourself with so much positivity and possibility that it overflows, leaving defeating thoughts in a huge cloud of smoke.

6. Letting go can be a powerful boost in the direction of your destiny.

RECOGNIZE DETOURS AS OPPORTUNITIES

On the road of life, we can be driving along smoothly, and from out of nowhere something hurdles in front of us unexpectedly. Sometimes we're so derailed by these hurdles that instead of continuing to drive toward success, we swerve away from our intended direction and wreck.

When this happens, some people stray from their path and become stagnant, never getting back on the right road. For others, they take a detour and end up at their desired destination—or a much better one. Some will do whatever it takes to remove the roadblock and get going again. Some will continue to stare at the roadblock and choose to do nothing, allowing fear and disappointment to stop them in their tracks. Whatever the case may be, it's important to remember that the road-blocks we all experience serve a purpose and that the universe is conspiring to give us what we want. The manner in which we interpret life's roadblocks and how well we're prepared to respond to them is crucial to our arrival on Success Street.

Maybe we were distracted and came up on a roadblock that could have been avoided. Sometimes, we are so distracted that we're not alert to what lies ahead, and we don't know how to appropriately react when we run up on those unexpected events and circumstances. Perhaps there have been times when road-blocks have gradually creeped into your path and, over a period of time, have decreased your vision and drivability without your being aware.

Roadblocks can come in various forms—some of them are clearly visible while others sneak up on you. Pull over and con-sider your own personal roadblocks. Awareness is the key to change. Could your roadblocks to emotional, physical, social, and financial success be in the form of a friend, family member, spouse, job, child, partner, etc.? Or could those roadblocks be parked in the corners of your mind in the form of self-doubt, worry, fear, anxiety, despair, loss, and defeat?

Most of the time, the anxiety we have while driving is the direct result of the "what if" scenarios that race through our minds and not because of what actually lies ahead. In reality, we are all fully equipped with the necessary tools to overcome life's obstacles based on the power that lies within our own minds. Not only are we manufactured to overcome life's roadblocks, but we are fully equipped to transform them into high-grade fuel on our journey.

So, what could be some potential roadblocks that are keeping you stalled on the road?

LOSS

We talked earlier about unresolved loss as being something that may be stored in your trunk that prevents you from moving forward. It can also be a major roadblock to various levels of emotional well-being and success. Sometimes, you'll experience the loss of things you desperately wanted, which can, then, create feelings of depression, disappointment, hopelessness, and despair. Grief is a normal human process that may include shock, denial, depression, and guilt. Ideally, acceptance is achieved at the end of the grieving process, enabling you to move forward with life despite your loss. Acceptance creates the fuel for you to reinvest in your own life without guilt and shame. Unfortunately, many people allow loss or unresolved grief to become a roadblock to living their full potential. The way you deal with this head-on is to acknowledge what is going on and give yourself permission to grieve. You must adopt the belief that moving on with your life is okay.

SELF-DOUBT

There's no greater roadblock to success than a negative self-perception. If you continuously put yourself down, minimize your accomplishments, think you're not good enough, and criticize yourself, you are creating the greatest barrier to your emotional well-being and overall success. Self-doubt can steer you toward failure if you allow it.

To achieve any goal, you must first *see* yourself achieving it. This is what you may have heard as seeing something in your "mind's eye." It is also your vision. If your "mind's eye" is seeing things that are not there or are not true, you are not getting a valid representation of reality, and you'll become paranoid of failure. If you expect to fail, you will. Instead of seeing what you get, you get what you see.

So, if you are picturing a negative outcome in your mind, you are most likely going to experience a negative outcome regardless of whether or not the reality could have been different.

Stop doubting yourself! Start fueling yourself with high-grade fuel! If you truly cannot allow yourself to come up with anything good about yourself, then focus on how you would *like* to be. Imagine all the characteristics and qualities you'd like to possess. Envision yourself possessing those qualities now. This clears the road for new possibilities. It also raises your vibrational frequency, which helps to bring good things to you instead of repelling them.

FEAR

Not only can fear cause you to blow smoke, it can also create major roadblocks in your life. Fear can rob you of your hopes and dreams and keep you living small. It's like having a new car and choosing to sit in the parking lot or garage where it's safe. It does nothing to serve you or move you toward your highest potential.

Consider FEAR to stand for "false evidence appearing real." Your mind doesn't recognize the difference between reality and imagination. If you believe it's real, then it is real to you! You will experience the same fearful emotions as you imagine to be true in your mind—even though what you're imagining may be completely false or unreal!

Remove the "fear shift" from your car, and replace it with the appropriate gearshift. Then, you can move forward with confidence and courage.

UNEXPECTED DETOURS

Perhaps you have created your own roadblock through a negative response to unexpected detours. Never underestimate the positive potential of a detour! If everything happened exactly the way we planned it, our lives would be limited to our expectations of the outcome. Detours can throw us off balance, frustrate and confuse us, and create anxiety about how to move forward if you let them. Detours can appear unexpectedly and force us to do something differently than we had originally planned. All too often, people give up when they have to detour from an original plan, never realizing the beauty and endless possibilities that the detour could serve to enrich their journey.

Anytime you see a "detour" road sign, you can bet it's been placed there for a significant reason and, more than likely, for your own protection. You must trust the process. Detours are put in our lives for a reason and are intended to have us take a different road—perhaps a much smoother road than the one we planned on traveling. Maybe it's a bumpier road than we ever imagined, but that was specifically designed to show you what you are really made of—in other words, to reveal how durable and tough you are!

Sometimes, detours help us find a better, faster route to our destination, but we would have never considered taking this new road on our own. Usually, once people get over the frustration, disappointment, and anxiety of a detour, they're able to look back and acknowledge their appreciation for it. Can you think of a detour that came into your life that may have caused a negative reaction in the beginning but ended up changing your life's journey for the better?

A detour that arises in your life has the power to create a wonderful journey or end one, depending on how you view it. Detours alone do not cause emotional reactions. It's the way you view and react to those detours that creates your emotions and corresponding behaviors. A detour is only a roadblock if you make it one. Start today making a conscious effort to see the unexpected detours that come into your life as a means of protection from harm and guidance to something better than you imagined for yourself.

Whether or not the roadblocks you are experiencing are set by you or something or someone else, here are some ways to get around them.

Be Still

If you unexpectedly come upon a roadblock, take a moment to be still. Clear your mind of the "what if" scenarios that create anxiety. Listen to your inner voice underneath the static. The best way to solve a problem comes in moments of stillness. If you have thoughts running a million miles a minute through your mind, it will cause things to become blurry. You'll be traveling at such a rapid rate of speed that you'll be unable to see the answers. Pull over, put your car in park, shut off the engine, and sit in silence. Make decisions from a place of peace and calmness rather than despair.

Search Your Own Vehicle

If you've come upon a roadblock and are unsure what to do, search your vehicle for the tools necessary to get around it. Look in your trunk for the items you have stored that will help you out in times of need, such as your shovel, duct tape, or booster cables. Utilize these things as needed in order to proceed. Look inside yourself for the strength and resiliency to keep moving on your journey despite what you have encountered.

Give Yourself a Sobriety Check

Check to see if you have been drinking from the bottle of negativity. Are you thinking about the roadblock with a clear mind? Are you able to drive in a straight line toward what you want, or are you allowing the roadblock to run you completely off course? There are always alternate routes to get around anything life throws at you. But, you must be mentally sober enough to formulate a sound plan of action. Otherwise, you could end up wrecked, killing your dreams.

Make Sure Your Driver's License Has Not Expired

Remind yourself that you've passed all requirements to hold a valid driver's license, allowing you to drive toward your goals. You were born to win! Successful driving does require renewal through maintenance and tune-ups, just as you must renew your driver's license periodically. However, no matter how old you are or what you've faced in life, your license to live a happy, productive, successful life never expires. You have a right to be happy. You have a right to be successful. Stop the flow of thoughts that revoke your ability to drive through life feeling good and achieving the things you desire.

Proceed with Caution

Once you've discovered a way to get back on the road, proceed with caution. Be alert to other potential roadblocks that could sneak up on you. It takes time and conscious effort to reprogram yourself. You have a lifetime of habits that may not have served you well, and it takes time to replace those habits. Drive forward with eager anticipation of what lies ahead, but continuously keep your thoughts in check.

Roadblocks can last a lifetime if you don't find successful ways to get around them or find ways to remove the ones that are created in your mind. Some people spend their entire lives making a permanent roadblock out of one that was only meant to be temporary. Your thoughts determine whether the roadblocks keep you stagnant or give you a boost in a new direction. Don't allow yourself to spin your wheels imagining the worst-case scenario from a temporary detour. Take some time to recharge, clean your windshield, and gas up to get around it. You will be surprised how much more efficient your car will run on this new road.

CHECKPOINTS

1. Awareness is the key to change and growth.

2. We are all fully equipped to overcome life's obstacles based on the power within our own minds.

3. Your license to live a happy, productive, successful life never expires.

4. Detours are encountered for a divine reason. You must trust the process.

5. Stillness brings answers. Slow down.

STAY IN YOUR LANE

When you are driving, how many times has your focus shifted to what is happening on the other side of the road? Most people could probably say this has happened to them at least once in their life, and if you are completely honest it has probably happened many times. Sometimes we become so focused on what's going on with the people around us that we tend to lose focus on what's going on within us.

There's a term that has been used to describe those who are turning their heads while driving to see who was pulled over by the police or to look at an accident that had occurred. It's called *rubbernecking*. Rubbernecking is not the way we should be spending our life! This keeps us from achieving what we are capable of and takes our attention away from where it needs to be in order to succeed. It steers us away from our own goals and desires while creating a sense of insecurity within ourselves.

When our attention shifts to what's going on in someone else's lane, we tend to swerve, run off the road, become distracted from our own path, and potentially end up spinning out of control. As a result of taking our eyes off the road *we're* traveling, it takes us longer to arrive at our destination—if we ever get there at all. Keeping our eyes on another's journey takes away our power train potential.

How many times have you compared yourself to someone else? How many times has this left you feeling insecure, less than, unattractive, or defeated? All too often, people look at others and their success and begin the downward spiral of negative self-talk, automatically putting their gearshift in park when it comes to making the effort to achieve the things they desire. The truth is, your journey is going to look much different than someone else's journey, and that's perfectly okay. It is not about them, it's about you and where you're going and the life you're creating for yourself.

Why would you even *want* to travel through life on someone else's journey anyway? Doing this will prevent you from experiencing the many opportunities available for your own personal growth and success. Stay focused on your own journey, and stop criticizing and comparing yourself to others! You can't get where you want to go in life if you're focused on what's going on in the southbound lane of the interstate. Get on the "inner-state" of your own well-being, and stay in that lane! Focus on where you're going and how far you have already come. In other words, stay in your lane so you don't end up emotionally wrecked!

Many people go through life comparing themselves to others. Perhaps you tell yourself you're not as talented or as smart as a friend, a sibling, or colleague. Maybe you feel like it's taking longer to accomplish a task that others around you seem to have accomplished in a shorter period of time, and because of this you've erroneously concluded that you're not capable.

Maybe you're comparing your make and model to others in that they seem brighter, better equipped, better polished, or more beautiful. Comparing yourself to others can leave you depressed, defeated, exhausted, and out of fuel. Comparisons can deflate your self-esteem and sense of self-worth. When you allow your perception of exterior things to dictate your driving abilities, you begin to destroy your own engine—the core component that gets you where you want to go in life. A V8 engine will never live up to its full potential if the driver barely presses the gas pedal and is under the impression that it'll only travel 25 miles per hour. We tend to live up to our own expectations. If you think your car will only get you so far, you'll stop there, never knowing where you could have gone.

Be informed that it's not about someone else's journey. It's about *your* journey! If everyone took the same route, there'd be no need for different roads! There is a quote that says, "Don't compare your chapter one to someone else's chapter twenty."

There are things that you'll learn on your journey that are specific to you—and only you. Sometimes, it's not about where you end up but what you have gone through and overcome to get there! It's about who you become in the process. Two people could leave the same location at the same time, go different routes, and end up at their destination hours or days apart. We must take into consideration that one person may have run into bad weather, or an accident, or a detour. For the person who encountered the delay, perhaps they were able to achieve great insight, increased patience, or something good that they would not have been led to if they traveled the same road as someone else.

Just as we need never doubt the power of a detour in life, we also should trust that our journey is meaningful and purposeful, and that it's okay, and even designed, for our journey to be unique. There are no time frames or specific routes to success as success can be achieved in the smallest of daily encounters and circumstances. All roads lead to somewhere, and it's important to trust that you're experiencing everything you need to experience that's meant for you—and only you. Let go of what's happening with others, and put the brakes on comparisons. It's crucial to stay in your lane while driving through life if you want to achieve success!

So how do you ensure that you don't become distracted by what's going on around you? How do you make sure you continue to stay centered in your own lane? Here are some examples to guide you along your way.

FOCUS

When you're driving, it's important to focus ahead. Be aware of your surroundings, but don't swerve toward every little distraction. Keep your focus on where you're going. Use your visions for your future as your guide. Don't get all bent out of shape over what's going on in the other lanes. Where you are now doesn't have to be where you stay. If you allow your focus to shift to another lane, your route becomes interrupted and can potentially lead to unexpected roadblocks that hinder success.

It's important not only to focus on the car directly in front of you but to continue to focus ahead to the horizon. If you're only focused on the car in front, you'll end up a follower. You could easily fall victim to their sudden stops and turns while losing sight of your dreams.

Drifting is caused by not looking far enough down the road. Don't drive aimlessly following someone else's lead. Don't allow someone else's opinion of you to change your direction. You know what you want, and you know where you want to go. Stay in your own lane while keeping your eyes focused ahead.

CHECK YOUR ALIGNMENT

A sure sign that your car is out of alignment is when it pulls to one direction and causes you to be unable to stay centered in your own lane. If you find that you're being pulled in the wrong direction, it's time to assess how well you are aligned with what you want. Consider this—you've taken your car to have your oil changed, and you have to pull onto the ramp to have your car lifted. If you do not align your wheels with the ramp, you will prevent yourself from receiving this important service.

As you set goals for yourself, you must regularly check to make sure you are aligned with them. By alignment, I mean keeping your thoughts positive, envisioning the outcomes you desire, maintaining the unswerving belief that you will accomplish your goals, and envisioning yourself at the finish line. You must mentally align yourself with thoughts and feelings of success and achievement. Align with people who lift you higher and inspire you to become the grandest version of yourself you can be!

CHECK YOUR MIRRORS BEFORE CHANGING LANES

If you want to avoid a head-on collision with other drivers, make sure you check your mirrors before changing lanes. Choosing to change lanes should be a well-thought-out, cautious maneuver. This is why side-view and rearview mirrors come standard on all automobiles. They're for your protection. When you're about to make a life-changing decision, you must use your mirrors to guide you. While it does not serve you to your highest potential to dwell on the past, acknowledging things in the past that didn't work for you can help you steer clear of repeated, unwanted experiences.

Sometimes we start out and then decide to take a different road. That's okay. We're free to change our direction anytime. If you decide to change lanes, make sure it's going to accelerate you toward your desired destination instead of away from it. Let your past experiences *guide* you, not *define* you.

LIMIT DISTRACTIONS

No matter where you're trying to go or what you're trying to accomplish in life, you can bet there'll be distractions that swerve over into your lane. Whether or not you allow them to run you off the road is up to you. What are the things that have been distracting you from your goals? What about your happiness and peace of mind? Who are the people who have distracted you? Are you one of them? What has caused you to steer off course? Distracted driving is a potentially deadly behavior! It can cost you everything! The greatest threat to your own safety on the road is you!

MERGE APPROPRIATELY

Traffic jams on highways are often triggered at the point two lanes merge into one. The best way to prevent traffic jams is to maintain enough space in front of your car to allow other cars to merge into your lane. Don't punish drivers for merging late. It's highly recommended that you encourage one, two, or even three cars to merge ahead of you.

On the road of life, we sometimes fall into the belief that there's not enough resources to supply all of us. People can fall into the belief that they must pass everyone up in order to arrive at the scarce amount of riches and success. The truth is, there's plenty of road space for all drivers, and it's unnecessary to exhibit any form of road rage in order to arrive at your own destination.

Zig Ziglar stated, "You can have everything in life you want if you will just help enough other people get what they want." Most people have it all wrong! They look at life and success in reverse. You can't get ahead by running other drivers off the road! The only person you should be trying to be better than is the person you saw in the mirror today—yourself!

What will you lose by assisting other drivers along the way? What could you gain? Would you appreciate someone else assisting you in times of need? When you gain the awareness that we're all trying to get somewhere and all of us have traveled some bumpy roads, you gain a sense of connectedness with others.

You may share the highway with certain people for a short period of time until they teach you what you need to learn about yourself and the world. Some people may travel alongside you your entire journey. The most important person you will ever travel with is yourself. You will have the most influence over whether or not you succeed. By success, I mean in whatever form it takes—mentally, physically, spiritually, interpersonally, financially, etc. Success means different things to different people. You must develop a clear picture of what success looks like to you, and then equip yourself with everything you'll need to achieve it.

Learn from past mistakes, but don't hold them out in front of you and allow them to defeat you. Be cautious when changing lanes, and don't chastise other drivers for their poor driving skills. Help others along the way. You get back what you give out! If you turn down Self-Centered Street, you'll arrive with nothing but your own ego and no one to support you when you need it. When you can truly be happy for others' success, you'll meet with your own! Allow space between you and other drivers when it comes time to merge. Trust that letting others enter your lane will not inhibit your progress but serve to speed it up.

In addition to the previous suggestions for staying in your lane, there may be times when you need to use defensive driving to keep from becoming involved in a wreck. A defensive driver is *proactive* rather than *reactive*. A good driver constantly takes in information and acts on it accordingly. Here are a few tips for defensive driving.

LOOK OUT FOR ROAD RAGE

More than likely, you've encountered what you would define as a driver with "road rage." This is someone who becomes angry if you make a minor driving error and who cuts you off, tries to race you, refuses to let you pass, or tailgates you. You may have even seen a "flying bird" a time or two from your front windshield or rearview mirror. Perhaps you've been the one to fly it?

Whatever the case, road rage is absolutely counterproductive to success! Aggression puts you on a negative frequency, and good cannot come to you if this is what you are sending out. Road rage drivers are often out to instigate trouble. Avoid getting into a confrontation with these drivers. Release attachment and further focus on the negative energy they project into your lane. This will ensure you arrive safely at your destination. If you respond in the same manner, you allow someone else to be in the driver's seat of your emotions and behaviors and, ultimately, your success.

GET AWAY FROM BAD DRIVERS

Perhaps other drivers on the road are not exhibiting road rage but are just simply bad drivers. These are drivers you must attempt to steer clear of as they could easily cause trouble for you and inhibit your progress. Keep a healthy distance between yourself and bad drivers on the road. Spending time too close to bad drivers is like hanging out with battery drainers. Stay in the lane with those who inspire and lift you higher and are flowing smoothly along through traffic. Follow those who motivate and help you accelerate. While it's recommended to assist other drivers along the way, you must also realize that unless the other driver wants assistance it's pointless.

DON'T FOLLOW TOO CLOSELY

Have you ever been driving and discovered someone is following so close to your bumper that if you tapped your breaks you'd get rear-ended? This can be especially problematic at night if someone has their high beams shining in your eyes through your rearview mirror and blinding you. This can lead to frustration and having to pull over to let them pass. Sometimes, it's necessary to pull over and let others pass—especially if they're creating distress and slowing you down.

It's okay to be passed, and it doesn't mean you're any less equipped or powerful than the person who passes you. Don't worry if others seem to be passing you in achieving their goals. Everyone is on their own journey, and if you continue to focus on what is going on in other lanes your journey will not be enjoyable and you will miss the meaning behind your experiences.

There may be times when you are following someone else too closely. Maybe you're right on their bumper, inhibiting yourself from moving forward at your own pace. Sometimes we doubt ourselves and feel much safer letting someone else take the lead. It may be easier to follow someone else's lead, but not stepping out of your comfort zone and taking the lead yourself will keep your gearshift stuck in park.

Who are you following? Do you have the desire to change lanes but fear of the unknown is stopping you from doing so? Maybe you don't trust your make and model to sustain your journey. Maybe you think your car is too old to make the journey. What if you break down? What if you get lost? All these "what ifs" can create enough anxiety to keep you a follower.

The truth is, you were born to be a leader! You have cutting-edge qualities that only you can offer the world, and you do yourself and others an injustice by driving in fear. Trust the process. Be your own roadside assistant. Muster enough courage to venture out onto unknown roads. Enjoy the ride!

SET AND KEEP YOUR BOUNDARIES

Imagine driving down the road with no painted lines. Lack of boundary lines could potentially cause collisions and accidents. It could lead to damaged cars that may have to be overhauled or completely parked.

Setting boundaries with others is crucial to your emotional, physical, and financial well-being. This means, if there's someone trying to get into your car and you don't want them along for the ride, you must assert yourself by telling them "no." Stop picking up hitchhikers if you don't want them to be part of your journey. Lack of boundaries is a significant reason people become frustrated, resentful, angry, and unmotivated. Can you identify boundaries that you need to set with others to decrease your negative emotional responses? How is not asserting yourself affecting your life? What is keeping you from setting boundaries?

Many times, lack of assertiveness and setting boundaries is due to underlying fear. Fear of losing people, making others upset, or damaging relationships. The reality of the situation is that if people cannot respect your boundaries, they are probably the battery drainers in your life that need to be removed. Even when you take the passive approach and go along with what you think they want, they're still draining your battery because you're likely doing things you don't want to do or not doing things you desire, which leads to harboring of resentment. Over time, this can ruin relationships—which is what people try to avoid by not setting boundaries with others.

The sad reality is, by not setting boundaries you are ruining a very important relationship—the one with yourself. Make sure your brake lights are working. You teach people how to treat you, and if they can't see your boundaries they'll run over you.

Now that you have been able to assess the lanes in which you're traveling, you can put an action plan into place as to how you'll proceed. By choosing to stay focused on your journey without making comparisons to others, checking your alignment and mirrors before switching lanes, limiting distractions so you don't swerve off course, making sure you merge appropriately, and not reacting to road rage, you further equip yourself for success.

CHECKPOINTS

1. Your journey is unique to you. Trust the process and stop making needless comparisons. They are a complete waste of valuable energy and will leave you emotionally wrecked.

2. Success is about who you become in the process. All detours and adversities are serving to create the grandest version of you.

3. If you are being pulled in various directions with limited progress, you are not aligned with what you want.

4. The most influential person in your life in terms of your success is you.

5. You have cutting-edge qualities that only you can offer the world. You do yourself and others a tragic injustice by driving in fear and playing small.

ADJUST YOUR FREQUENCY

Many people enjoy cruising down the highway listening to their favorite radio station. Perhaps you have a favorite station you like to tune in to while you drive. There's something about this music that speaks to your inner being and leaves you feeling energized, inspired, relaxed, and happy. You probably even have this station programmed into your radio so that, with the simple touch of a button, you can tune in to what you want to hear. You know this is the right station for you because it makes you feel good. You may even sing along to the music. Maybe there are certain stations you never tune to because they drive you crazy or make you cringe. The last thing you want to end up doing is singing along to one of these stations.

You have complete control over the station you hear—unless you're riding in the backseat of your own or another's car. In this case, you're at someone else's mercy—that is, until you assert yourself by speaking up, making a request, getting out of the car, or taking the wheel and kicking someone else out of your car.

Some people drive through life tuned to a station they don't like, feeling helpless to make changes. Some may not even be driving at all, but are a passive passenger in their own car. It's as if they are saying to themselves that this is the station that was playing when they got in the car, so that is the station they are destined to listen to.

The point is, you have so much more power over your life than you realize! There's absolutely no reason you can't get into the driver's seat and steer your life in any direction you want! You don't have to drive through life tuned to the wrong station—and you do have the power to change it! But first, you must understand how it all works.

Perhaps you perceive a radio as simply something you listen to. But in reality, it's so much more! Maybe you perceive life as something that happens "to" you instead of something that happens "for" you. "Radio" means sending energy waves. The equipment that sends out radio waves is called the "transmitter." Waves sent by the transmitter travel through the air and reach their destination when meeting with a second piece of equipment called the "receiver."

You see, when you tune in to a radio station, there's an electric circuit inside the radio that selects only the program you want from all those that are broadcasting. This is how it also works with your thoughts and where you choose to focus your energy and attention. There's a quote that says, "Energy flows where attention goes." Your car will end up wherever you turn your steering wheel and your attention. If you find yourself stuck in a ditch or stranded beside the road, it's time to refocus and turn your wheel in a different direction.

Consider yourself as both the transmitter and the receiver. You receive what you tune to as well as what you transmit to yourself. What happens when we are broadcasting a negative frequency? How do others receive what we are transmitting, and how does this directly impact our relationships? What about our lives?

What we send out returns to us. If you're transmitting negative energy, you can be assured you'll have head-on collisions with more negative experiences. Then, by choosing to tune your attention to those negative experiences, you receive even more negative feelings and experiences. The important and perhaps most crucial thing to realize is that at any point you can change your frequency and change your life experiences.

Frequency is defined as the rate at which something occurs or is repeated over a period of time. It can also be defined as the rate at which a vibration occurs that constitutes a wave either in material (as sound waves) or an electromagnetic field (as radio waves), usually measured per second. If you don't like the station, stop listening to it over and over again. Make a conscious choice to find a new station that makes you feel better when you hear it. Darryl Anka stated, "Everything is energy and that's all there is to it. Match the frequency of the reality you want and you cannot help but get that reality. It can be no other way. This is not philosophy. This is physics."

Every thought carries its own vibrational frequency. Everything emits a frequency—even an atom. If you desire to stay upbeat and energetic and encounter positive life experiences, think positive thoughts. If you find yourself feeling down, defeated, and hopeless, you're thinking thoughts that alter your vibrational frequency.

You can judge your frequency by your mood as it is directly influenced by the thoughts you think. Frequency is measured by a unit called "hertz." So, you can count on the fact that if it "hertz" to hear it, you need to change the station!

Each morning when you wake up, you choose what station you tune in to. It is said that the first five minutes after we awaken dictate our day. The most powerful tool you are equipped with as a human being is your ability to choose your own thoughts. You may not be able to choose everything that happens to you in life, just as you cannot control the multitude of signals broadcasted across the air waves, but you *can* choose what you tune in to and how you react. This equipment comes standard on all vehicles, but not everyone knows how to use this key feature. You can also choose to believe that events do not happen *to* you, they happen *for* you. You can use *any* life experience for your good and the good of others. However, those experiences can fool you or fuel you.

Through awareness of your thoughts and by fine-tuning your frequency, you ensure you can remain in the driver's seat of your life—regardless of which road you travel. Guard your frequency like an antitheft device on your car. If you hear the alarm sounding within you, it's time to take action before someone else either steals valuable parts of you or drives off with your car. Be vigilant! Don't allow this to happen! You are already equipped to prevent this, but you must realize your power and apply it for success.

Okay. Now, let's examine the difference between AM, FM, and digital in terms of radio stations.

THE FREQUENCY OF AM

AM stands for "amplitude modulation." *Amplitude* is a measurement that indicates the movement or vibration of something. It can also be defined as the extent of dignity, excellence, or splendor and the quality or state of being ample, full, and abundant. How many times have you said to yourself, "*I am…*?" Perhaps you do not currently realize the power of these two words. If you want to reach your goals and desired destination, it's essential that you see yourself the way you want to be and visualize yourself living the life you desire. You can't define yourself from a point of lack and manifest abundance. If you see yourself from the point of prosperity, you will prosper!

Again, this is matching your frequency to the reality you want. Preset your station to what you want to hear or want to experience. Perhaps a new station may be the "I am unstoppable" station, the "I am a powerful creator" station, or any other "*I am*" station you would like. Just as you wouldn't stay tuned to a station that isn't pleasing to you, you must not stay tuned to a thought frequency that is displeasing and steers you off the road of success, happiness, and peace of mind. By setting and listening to your particular AM station, you fuel yourself with courage, strength, resiliency, power, motivation, determination, perseverance, and passion for your journey. As a result, you'll live life with dignity, excellence, splendor, and abundance!

FM RADIO

In case you're not familiar with the way FM radio works, I'll provide you with a brief overview. Radio waves carry energy as an invisible, up and down movement of electricity and magnetism. Program signals are carried from huge transmitter antennas connected to both the radio station and the smaller antenna on your radio. A program is transmitted by a radio wave called a "carrier," and this process is called "modulation." When a radio program is added to the carrier in such a way that the program signal causes fluctuations in the carrier's frequency, this is called *frequency modulation* (FM).

Let's define FM fluctuations in the frequencies *you* transmit and receive. These fluctuations directly impact your mood and behavior and influence whether you arrive on Success Street or Failure Avenue. Frequency is attained by thinking high-energy thoughts and focusing on them frequently with strong emotion.

Remember, a negative frequency is created by continually focusing on negative thoughts. Whatever you consistently think about drives your emotions. Many people continue down the same dead-end street, never realizing all they have to do is to turn the wheel and take a different route. It's like listening to the same station repetitively and becoming tired of the same old song and the interference and static but never changing the station. This is when you end up on Insanity Street—driving down the same street over and over and wondering why you are never able to make it to a different location. It's simply not going to happen!

What you focus on drastically impacts your life, so proceed with caution when choosing your thoughts. Be intentional with your thinking! Don't drive through life not recognizing how you got where you are now. Know precisely where you're going, and pay attention along the way. You are fueled by your thoughts! What you think about will continue to show up in your life experience.

When you find yourself thinking about things that are negatively affecting your frequency—such as all the ice holes you have run into—you must take immediate action. You may have to swerve to miss debris lying in the middle of the road. Don't allow your car to be damaged or wrecked by someone else's garbage. The more you practice intentional self-detouring, the more likely you are to have a happy and fulfilled life.

DIGITAL RADIO

Digital radio promises almost perfect sound. While most digital radio systems are typically designed for handheld mobile devices, some provide in-band, on-channel solutions that may coexist or simulcast with AM or FM transmissions. If you want to enhance your life's journey and ensure you end up where you want to go, you should incorporate all three forms of radio.

Digital radio ensures that no matter what may come between your radio and transmitter, the signal almost always gets through. This is why digital radio sounds better. Another unique feature of digital radio is that you can pause a live broadcast and restart it later. How do you suppose your life could be different if you practiced pausing and restarting the thoughts you think or even, potentially, some of your behaviors? This would bring more awareness to the types of thoughts you're thinking and create conscious thinking.

In other words, you'll deliberately choose your thoughts and, by doing so, steer your life in the direction you want. If you find yourself starting down the wrong road, pause and restart with better thoughts and behaviors that will serve as fuel for your journey. Don't expect to master this immediately. It takes time to reprogram thought patterns, so be patient. Consider it like driver's education class or perhaps better stated as thinker's education class.

One of the greatest things about a receiver with digital radio is that it can take fragments arriving from various places and reassemble them, thereby creating an uninterrupted program signal. Start piecing together all the positive things people have said to you and all the joyous events you are grateful to have experienced. Allow yourself to feel good about all of these positive events. When you consciously take time to steer your attention toward good-feeling thoughts and memories, you strategically and intentionally raise your vibrational frequency. This is a sure way to tune to a station that will make you want to sing along.

Now that you're more knowledgeable about the different types of radio stations and how they operate, let's examine other key components of your car's radio system that are beneficial to getting the best overall reception.

RECEIVER

A radio receiver is an electronic device that receives radio waves and converts the information carried by them to a usable form. The information produced by the receiver may be in the form of sound, images, or data. Again, you are both the transmitter and receiver of your own messages—the things you repeat continually to yourself. Not only are you both the transmitter and the receiver of the signals you send, but you are the receiver of others' transmissions as well. How affected you are by others' words and actions is determined by how you let them filter through your mind.

Think back to the items stored in your trunk that have continued to replay in your mind and weighed you down and kept you from achieving your true potential. Think of the specific words someone said to you that changed your frequency to a station you didn't like. Maybe this is the station you have remained tuned to most of your life. You received those words and then filtered what you focused on.

Once you choose a station, you then become the transmitter as well by repeating those same things to yourself. Has anyone ever told you that you would never be able to do or accomplish something or that you're unworthy of success? If so, have you ever repeated these same lies to yourself and then begun to believe them?

Hopefully, now you have a clearer picture of how this works. If you do, then you are also beginning to tune in to how much power you have over your life. Remember, anything can be broadcasted from another transmitter, but you have a choice as to how—and whether or not—you receive it.

AMPLIFIERS

Amplifiers magnify sound waves. They provide an extra boost to enhance the signal being transmitted. The amplifier is a small chip that boosts signal strength to make it powerful enough to drive a loudspeaker. What kind of things do you tend to amplify that will become your life experience? Are you spending your mental energy amplifying the negatives or the positives? What you amplify comes out of your loudspeaker.

Let's consider your loudspeaker to be verbalized thoughts—perhaps your "I am" thoughts that you outwardly project. You are constantly transmitting messages to yourself and others. Make sure your thoughts reflect what you want to hear and that they accelerate you in the right direction.

SPEAKERS

The speakers in a car take an electrical signal provided by the head unit and convert it into sound. It is said that a proper head unit should be able to power speakers adequately in order to use them to their full potential. The head unit also adjusts the pitch and frequency output for the speakers. If you don't have your head in the right place, you're likely to speak to both yourself and others in ways you are likely to regret later.

Let's say there's a brand-new car sitting on an automobile dealer's sales lot. The salesperson comes out and describes the car as used, dented, wrecked, and likely to break down beside the road. Most people, if not all, would never consider investing in that type of car. The perception would be that it's a piece of junk. However, the reality is that it's a new car with limitless potential that could take you anywhere you wanted to travel.

If you speak ill of yourself, others are not likely to believe in you even though you are perfectly capable of achieving great things. If you do not believe in yourself, others are not likely to believe in you either. If you don't believe you can drive, you will never get behind the wheel. You will let life experiences and others steer you wrong.

Therefore, speak words of encouragement, abundance, strength, prosperity, and faith to yourself and others. Remember, the words projected from your speakers are coming directly from the station you are tuned to. If something is displeasing to hear, hit the mute button and change the station before speaking. Speak only of how you want things to be instead of the way you perceive things to be—unless you like the way things currently are. The more you speak of something, the more you will experience it. Speak of things that are pleasing to you. This will then be a station you'll want to listen to! Stop accepting more of the same, or should I say stop creating more of the same! Your words become your life. You speak your own reality, and that is powerful!

TRANSFORMER

The transformer's function in a car radio is to scale down the AC voltage so it's safe and appropriate for the radio's delicate components. A series of smaller transformers help the radio hone in on the specific station you want by blocking out other nearby stations. You have the built-in ability to transform your life. The key is recognizing your true potential and practicing fine-tuning.

It can be difficult to block out hurtful things others have said or done to us. It's unlikely we will ever totally forget these things, but we don't have to continue to waste energy and attention on them. You can choose to tune out this station and refuse to let it affect your entire life. There will always be numerous stations broadcasting around you as you travel through life. However, when you master the art of fine-tuning, you transform your life. When you learn to use other stations that have interfered with yours as fuel for your journey, you will drive yourself straight to success. You become an unstoppable, unshakable vessel!

CHECKPOINTS

1. Life doesn't happen "to" you; it happens "for" you.

2. At any point you can change your frequency and thus change your life experiences.

3. The most powerful tool you are equipped with is the power to choose your thoughts.

4. You can't define yourself from a point of lack and manifest abundance.

5. You are both the transmitter and the receiver of your own messages. Choose wisely.

Make a "You" Turn to Fulfill Your Inner Drive

It's probably safe to say that at some point in time we have all become unhappy with certain areas of our lives. Perhaps you're experiencing burnout and find it difficult to have motivation and enthusiasm to continue with your current life or job responsibilities. Perhaps you're unhappy with yourself.

For many, it's easy to recognize unhappiness and loss of enthusiasm, but it's much more difficult to turn around, change gears, and go in another direction. If you have ever driven a five-speed automobile, you understand that you must sometimes change gears as you accelerate or decelerate. You cannot move forward or backward without doing so. Also, if you get stuck in between gears, the engine will rev and the car will jerk until you find the right gear. The car will let you know when you've missed the gear and/or something is not quite right. Your body and emotions will let you know when things are not right. Then, it's time to make a "you" turn!

Sometimes we experience headaches, stomachaches, back-aches, anxiety, or depression. We may become hard on ourselves by only focusing on the negatives, which leads us to lose motivation and interest to invest in daily life activities. Sometimes we just simply don't know how to change the gears appropriately to make our lives run more smoothly.

Unfortunately, we may become accustomed to driving through life on automatic—just driving aimlessly in directions that are not good for us. Sometimes we are so focused on failing that we choose to drive at the slow speed with which we are comfortable and, therefore, never really put forth the effort to accelerate or take a new road that will lead us to our full potential.

We choose the roads we travel, and those roads dictate what we see and experience. If you don't like your current scenery, make a "you" turn and go in a different direction! Choose to go in the direction that most reflects what you desire for your life. Many times, this requires a shift in your perspective. Your circumstances and situations do not have to change for you to take the wheel and start enjoying the scenery. The only requirement is a change in the way you think about those circumstances and situations. When you shift perspective, it's like putting a brand new frame on an old picture. A nice frame can make the picture look a whole lot better even though the picture itself didn't change. Don't let fear of the unknown or of making a wrong decision keep your gearshift in neutral or park.

Have the courage to shift out of first gear and change direction! Don't be afraid of getting lost. You are only lost if you see yourself as such. All roads lead to somewhere! You just have to find the road that will take you where you want to go. Don't be afraid of missing the right gear—just keep trying. Realize that it's not only okay but essential that you take care of yourself. You know better than anyone else your desires and aspirations. If you're on the road that others are dictating to you, it's time to turn around and make your journey about you! Sometimes, being jerked around might be exactly what you need to fuel your desire for success. If you keep traveling down the same road and you hate it, the answer is as clear as a freshly cleaned windshield—change direction and make a "you" turn!

Have you ever been driving along and something catches your eye and all of a sudden you start driving in that direction, perhaps running off the road or crossing into the median? We go in the direction of our thoughts. They are like the steering wheel of our car. Where we turn it, the car follows. What direction are you turning your wheel? What scenery are you getting distracted by? Are you focused more on negativity or positivity? Whichever one is true for you is what you will continue to experience until you change the direction of your mind.

Your current scenery does not determine your journey or final destination. Sometimes people get so caught up in current circumstances that they don't see a way out. There's always a way out! There's always a different route. It's never too late to do what is best for you. If you continue looking at the dead-end street sign, you're unable to see other avenues that lead to success. You must shift gears, turn around if necessary, and start a new journey. In what areas do you need to change direction?

Perhaps you have identified some areas where you need to shift gears and change your direction. It's wonderful if you've come to this realization and finally admitted this to yourself. Recognition and admission is the first step! Shift the energy you once spent dwelling on the negatives to focus on where you're going and the wonderful things that are to come. Keep your eyes focused ahead! Now you can get out of first gear and turn your wheels.

This would be a great time to pull out the tools you have stored in your trunk to help you through this process. Shovel out the negativity and surround yourself with only positive people who encourage you. Apply imaginary duct tape to those who criticize or doubt you and duct tape the negative, self-defeating things you say to yourself. It's time for a "you" turn!

Now is your time to put yourself first. It's your turn to be happy. It's your turn to experience the life you've imagined. It's your turn to be in the driver's seat and disregard direction from backseat drivers.

Are you one of those people who have spent their entire lives taking care of others and neglecting yourself? It's wonderful to assist others, but it's not beneficial to neglect yourself! By neglecting yourself, you're shortchanging others from experiencing the best version of you.

Have you stalled in setting goals for yourself because of guilt about not devoting your time and energy to others? Has the road you've been traveling headed the opposite direction from the life you truly desire? If so, it's definitely a sign it's time for a "you" turn.

A "you" turn is an intentional turn in the opposite direction from which you've been traveling. There are no illegal "you" turns on the road of life. You can take this action wherever and whenever you choose. "You" turns are different from U-turns on the highways. U-turns can only be made at traffic lights where there is a U-turn permitted sign. In life, you must give yourself permission to do this whenever you feel the need to do so.

"You" turns help develop your authentic self. This is the "you" at your core. When you come into alignment with who you really are, you establish the grandest version of yourself to offer the world. Your journey becomes beautiful no matter what's happening around you—not to mention the full experience of happiness, contentment, peace, and joy you have so long desired.

U-turns are usually made because you are going the wrong direction or you need to go back to get something. Isn't it time you go and find yourself? Isn't it time to recreate yourself?

How many times have you been driving, knowing you're headed the wrong direction, but passed up many opportunities to change direction? What kept you from turning around? Was it fear of being reprimanded or fear of embarrassment? What's keeping you from turning around at this moment? Have you been hearing that knocking sound from underneath your hood that's indicating to you that something isn't right? If so, this is the "real" you trying to get your attention! Listen closely to your inner self! Sometimes you may have to cut the car off and sit in silence to hear the message your true self is trying to tell you. Stop ignoring it!

All those times you found yourself disappointed with life and yourself and all those times you felt that things were not working out as you'd planned, they really were working in your favor! All these experiences were necessary to develop you and to help you realize who you really are and what you really want.

When the direction you are going is the exact opposite of where you really want to go, you encounter inner conflict and dis-ease with life. You stop running smoothly. You start stalling. Your car starts to fall apart piece by piece until there's nothing left but the body.

Lack of direction or traveling in the wrong direction can weaken your spirit and break you down. The longer you continue to drive in the wrong direction, the worse it gets. You end up driving through life in a four-cylinder car that feels like it's trying to pull a tractor trailer behind it. You travel through life exhausted and worn. A much needed "you" turn can completely change your life for the better. Once you make this choice, you'll wonder why in the world you didn't do it sooner! However, it wasn't meant to happen then; it is meant to happen now! Perhaps you needed the experiences of the journey you've been on to fully equip you to get to this point of action. There are no wrong turns, only character-building avenues.

No one knows you better than you! Stop allowing others to define you and steer you away from your purpose. Put your foot on the brake and make that "you" turn. Right here, right now, in the middle of the road! Stop programming yourself to believe that you have traveled too far to go a new direction. It's not too late! No, it's *never* too late as long as there's life in your body!

CHECKPOINTS

1. If you continue looking at a dead-end street, you will be unable to see other avenues for success.

2. Stop ignoring your inner self. Consider it your internal GPS.

3. A "you" turn is an intentional turn in the opposite direction from the one you've been traveling. Is it time to make one for yourself?

4. When the direction you are going is the exact opposite of where you really want to go, you encounter inner conflict and dis-ease with life.

TAKE THE WHEEL AND DRIVE YOURSELF SUCCESSFUL!

Hopefully, you have now gained awareness of what items need to be cleaned out of your trunk and what to replace them with that will ensure a successful journey. You've begun filling yourself with high-grade thoughts to use as fuel; started giving yourself necessary tune-ups; have made the decision to engage in regular maintenance; reignited your spark; developed a clear vision of what you want; stopped blowing smoke and started taking action toward achievement of your desires; changed your thoughts about detours; started removing the roadblocks you have set for yourself; centered yourself in your lane; adjusted your frequency; and have decided to make a "you" turn. Now, it's time to take the wheel and drive to success! You've gained a newfound grip on life and are discovering who you really are on a highway filled with endless possibilities.

No more yielding to self-defeating thoughts, comparisons, past failures, lack of self-care, and criticism from others. No more allowing past experiences to keep you from being who you're meant to be. You are now in the driver's seat of your own life! Doesn't it feel good? Take a moment to absorb the magnificence of this. Isn't it amazing to realize that you held the key this entire time? You're free to travel anywhere with complete control over your response to any potential distractions you may encounter. You're fully equipped to triumph over any potholes you come across on your journey. You have a mind-set for success. Your time is *now!* Can you hear and feel your engine revving? You're ready to go!

It doesn't matter how long it's taken you to get to this point because you are exactly where you are meant to be at this moment. Everything about your journey is unfolding perfectly. You are in alignment with your desires. Feel how good this feels! Allow yourself to feel the way you anticipate feeling when you achieve your dreams. Feel it now! This will get you on the right frequency to receive all you've ever wanted—to arrive at everything you have programmed into your GPS. Go ahead and express gratitude as if you have already achieved what you want! Gratitude in advance accelerates you toward success and the attainment of your desires.

Grip your steering wheel tight, and keep looking out your windshield! Continue looking forward. Let your vision guide you. Hold on to it relentlessly, for it's the road map to your life's coming attractions. Even if it's too foggy to see in front of you right now and even if you become blinded by other drivers, keep driving! Look within yourself for answers and guidance. Listen to your inner voice. It will let you know when you are traveling in the wrong direction. The fog *will* clear. If you lose sight, keep driving because you will eventually regain it. By not stopping, you continue to make progress toward your desires.

You are the assertive driver of your life. Don't take a backseat to anyone. Maybe it's time to stop and let some people out. Not everyone is meant to ride with you your entire journey. That's okay. Recognize that everyone has served their purpose for helping you arrive at your authentic self. Let them off the hook for all the wrongs you perceive they have done to you. Instead of seeing them as driving you mad, you can now say they drove you to success! Shift gears to expressing gratitude for them helping to polish you into the person you are meant to be. Use your rearview mirror periodically as a guide, but don't let what you see behind you define you. Every day is a new day, a fresh start. Refuse to go back and pick up things that used to be stored in your trunk that you've cleared out. There's absolutely nothing back there that has the power to dictate your future. Stop looking back because you are no longer traveling that road.

Now that you've decided to take the wheel, you have complete control over how you deal with unexpected detours. Remember, not only are you manufactured to overcome life's detours, you are fully equipped to transform them into high-grade fuel for your journey to greatness!

By realizing that we are all constantly under construction, the detours and bumps in the road become much more passable. You can now make a conscious choice to refrain from creating roadblocks for yourself from the unexpected turns of life. Take the detours and embrace every mile! Be open to observing the beauty in all situations and know that they each carry the seed of a greater benefit. There is always a silver lining. It's up to you to find it!

Every single experience, hardship, defeat, failed relationship, loss, and disappointment has prepared you for the present moment. Drive forward with a tank full of gratitude for these things. Continue to fuel yourself with "I am" statements and set your frequency for success. For every mile marker you pass, remind yourself you are capable, equipped, powerful, and worthy. You were created to fulfill your destiny, and you have what it takes!

Program the stations you want to hear while you drive, and cruise down the highway listening to the stations that make you happy and confident. The music you listen to has the power to change your mood, so choose your stations wisely. It's time to start singing along to a new song. If you don't like what you are hearing, change the station and reprogram. If you don't like the direction you're going, make a "you" turn right in the middle of the road. You can do that at any point in life!

Refuse to settle for a curbside life. Refuse to stand outside your car only wishing you could take it for a spin. Take the wheel of opportunity! Take the wheel and drive away in faith. Take the wheel of your happiness, health, wealth, and well-being! Take the wheel of your relationships. Take the wheel, and be willing to go an extra mile. Take the wheel of your success and your life! You are in complete control over your own happiness, and it's totally up to you to experience it!

This book has returned your keys and shown you how to get back into the driver's seat of life. Refuse to doubt yourself and your abilities ever again! When you recognize your own strength, resilience, operating abilities, power train potential, and adapt an unswerving positive attitude, you obtain success!

About Rachel Lynn

Rachel Lynn is a professional speaker, Director of the Center for Student Development, licensed professional counselor, Director of the Napoleon Hill Scholars program, and professor of Napoleon Hill's "Keys to Success" course at the University of Virginia's College at Wise. Rachel is certified in Clinical Supervision with the Virginia Board of Counseling, in Glutenology with the Gluten Free Society, and is a Certified Law of Attraction Basic Practitioner with the Global Sciences Foundation. Rachel has presented at the Virginia Counselors' Convention in Hot Springs, Virginia; American Counseling Association's National Conference in Pittsburgh, Pennsylvania; the Help, Hope, and Healing Conference in Big Stone Gap, Virginia; as well as numerous other settings on the topics of self-care, mental health, personal development, motivation, gluten sensitivity, and mindfulness.

Rachel is a member of the American Counseling Association, American College Counseling Association, and the Concerned about Our Community Coalition. Rachel was a featured guest on "Journey to Success" blog talk radio and was personally invited to attend "Secret Knock" in San Diego, California. Here she was able to directly network with best-selling authors, inspirational speakers, entrepreneurs, etc. Rachel is passionate about inspiring and motivating others to achieve optimal well-being and success.